ABOUT THE AUTHOR

Erik Skare is an activist and editor for the pro-Palestinian website Infofada. He is also the author (in Norwegian) of *Palestine: A Political Travel Guide*.

DIGITAL JIHAD

PALESTINIAN RESISTANCE IN THE DIGITAL ERA

Erik Skare

ZED

Zed Books

LONDON

Digital Jihad: Palestinian resistance in the digital era was first published in 2016 by Zed Books Ltd, The Foundry, 17 Oval Way, London SE11 5RR, UK.

www.zedbooks.net

Typeset in Adobe Garamond Pro by seagulls.net
Index by John Barker
Cover design by Michael Oswell

A catalogue record for this book is available from the British Library.

ISBN 978-1-78360-785-3 hb
ISBN 978-1-78360-784-6 pb
ISBN 978-1-78360-786-0 pdf
ISBN 978-1-78360-787-7 epub
ISBN 978-1-78360-788-4 mobi

*Dedicated to Jon Børge Hansen
and the rest of the old guard.*

CONTENTS

ACKNOWLEDGMENTS

I owe a debt of gratitude to many people for helping bring this book to fruition.

First of all, my main supervisor for the research on which this book is based, Associate Professor Albrecht Hofheinz, introduced me to the topic of Arab hacktivists and hacking in the Middle East several years ago at the University of Oslo. I have benefited enormously from his vast knowledge of the Internet and its development in the Middle East.

I also owe great gratitude to my secondary supervisor, Professor Brynjar Lia. I consider myself blessed to have worked for him while writing this book, and he is in many ways my academic role model. Both Hofheinz and Lia gave me invaluable advice and constructive criticism, but most importantly encouragement and moral support through the whole process. I am forever indebted for their input.

Professor at the University of Oslo, Berit Thorbjørnsrud, was of immense help. Her keen eye for the smallest details and longer lines was invaluable and this book would not have been the same without her. Also Charlotte Lysa and Miriam Chakroun were of great help.

The same applies to all of the wonderful people working at the Department of Culture Studies and Oriental Languages at the University of Oslo who gave their time to discuss even the smallest details of the topic. I am also grateful for what they have done, intentionally or not, to create a safe work environment that makes people dare to fail – and thus, subsequently, to succeed.

Anne Stenersen, research fellow at the Norwegian Defense Research Establishment, has during my time there become (rather unwillingly) a mentor and a good friend. I will never stop being amazed by her knowledge of radical Islamism, jihadism and the Internet. She gave me invaluable help with this book and I am tremendously grateful for her input. She is truly a brilliant woman.

Reema Asia was always there to help me with new perspectives, ideas and ways to approach the political aspects of this book. She is one of the strongest and brightest Palestinian women I know.

Per Atle Pedersen paid for dinners and an unhealthy amount of coffee while discussing the political and technological aspects of this book. Steinar Pedersen, Gullbrand Giacobbe-Helleberg and Ole Egge are also, alongside Per Atle, a part of the old guard to which this book is dedicated.

Both Peder Martin Lysestøl, associate professor at Sør-Trøndelag University College, and Petter Bauck of the Norwegian Agency for Development Cooperation (NORAD) offered necessary comments on the principal political ideas of this book and corrections on even the smallest details. My good friend Magne Hagesæter helped me with the book, and what he does not know about the Palestinian issue is not worth knowing. Also, my sister-in-law Kamilla was of immense help in structuring the arguments and clarifying the answers to the questions I was posing.

My editor, Kim Walker, deserves a special thank you for supporting me and believing in this book; she is the best editor anyone could wish for. Also, I am truly grateful to the book's peer reviewer for setting the bar so high. It has improved the book in ways I could not imagine.

I am indebted to my girlfriend Mathilde, who not only read the manuscript several times and provided me with invaluable feedback, but also encouraging me to continue writing when I felt I could not go on.

Finally, I am grateful for the help and support of my parents. Not only with this book, but all the years they have read, commented and corrected everything that I have written. This book would not have been completed without them. Especially my mother, professor at the University of Tromsø, spent too many hours reading the manuscript and provided me with more or less useful resources. The same applies to my father, who could have been an excellent scholar and academic. He has chosen to enjoy life instead.

Flaws and inaccuracies that have slipped through are my responsibility alone.

This book was written with the financial help of Norsk Faglitterær Forfatter- og Oversetterforening (Norwegian Non-Fiction Writers and Translators Organization).

EDITORIAL NOTE

TRANSLITERATIONS

This book uses the transliteration standard of the *International Journal of Middle East Studies* (IJMES), which is considered as one of the leading standards for Arabic transliteration to the Latin alphabet. When addressing Arabic words and sentences – regarding the most important differences from simplified transliteration – I render the letters *ayn* (ع) as '‘', *hamza* (ا) as '’', *dha* (ظ) as 'ẓ', *ta* (ط) as 'ṭ', *ha* (ح) as 'ḥ', *saad* (ص) as 'ṣ', and *ta marbūta* (ة) as 'a' and in constructions '-at'.

Long vowels (ى, ي and و) are transliterated in the following order as 'ā', 'ī', and 'ū'. Doubled (يّ and وّ) are in the following order transliterated as 'iyy', with the final 'ī', and 'uww', with the final 'ū'. Diphthongs are transliterated as 'ay' (ي) and 'aw' (و). *Hamzat al-Waṣl* is not written.

For the names of persons, I have given the names in full transliteration. When there is a commonly understood way of writing names in English – as with Fatah, Hamas, and Mahmoud Abbas – no transliteration is given.

NAMES AND ANONYMIZATION

Several of the sources in this book – from the fieldwork in the West Bank, interviews with hackers, and conversations with sources in the Norwegian intelligence services – have been anonymized. This first of all applies to the Palestinians willing to discuss several aspects but who face a military occupation, with all of the dangers that it entails. The same applies to those in the Norwegian intelligence services, who do not face the same repercussions as the Palestinians but nevertheless should not have their careers jeopardized. If there has been any doubt about the necessity of anonymization, I have followed the principle of better safe than sorry.

PROLOGUE

"So, are you still in touch with them?"

I found myself in a small room, no larger than 3 by 4 meters, in front of two officers, an old man and a slightly younger woman, from the Norwegian National Security Authority (NNSA), one of three Norwegian secret service bureaus. They had questions, a lot of questions. Specifically about my fieldwork for my master's thesis, and the Palestinian groups I had been in touch with in the West Bank and online – the Palestinian Islamic Jihad, Hamas and Gaza Hacker Team. I was participating in a joint project between the University of Oslo and the Norwegian Defense Research Establishment as a research assistant to create an online depository comprising of jihadist primary sources and therefore I needed security clearance.

"Well, actually, I am." I put on some kind of grin to show that it was not a big deal. "I sent Gaza Hacker Team my master's thesis today. I mean, we had a deal that I would do so to make sure that I actually was a master's student at the University of Oslo. It was a token of trust."

The man, looking like a rather less charming and slightly taller Danny DeVito, and the other lady, who did not do much more than vigorously write down everything that I said, did not give any sign of caring about my replies. "I want to know more about the Palestinian Islamic Jihad. How did you get in touch with them?" He looked at me in a way so uncomfortable it forced me to look away for a second.

"Well, I will not give you any names, but—"

"Why?!" For the first time during the whole interrogation he actually raised his voice and stared at me.

I tried to stay calm as I answered, "Because they are in a situation where they are in danger of being imprisoned, tortured, killed, and—"

Once again he interrupted me, "And who would possibly do that!?"

"The Israelis, of course", I replied. "It has been documented several times by Israeli human rights groups such as B'Tselem that torture is being conducted in Israeli prisons."

"All right, but we want to know exactly how you met them? How did you get in touch with them?"

I was at this point thinking carefully how I could possibly give them information to such a degree that I was not deemed "unwilling to cooperate" at the same time as not giving them any information that could possibly put my sources at risk: "You know, I have been in Palestine multiple times for the last eight years. You always know someone who knows someone. I met a person, I asked to meet Islamic Jihad, and he called his contact who called another contact. A couple of days later I received a message and a meeting was set up."

"I think it is best we move on…" He seemed annoyed. "Did you talk about the Arab spring in Egypt with your Hamas contacts?"

I was suddenly dumbfounded by the question and it was all I could think about as I walked out of their massive building in the middle of Oslo. How did they know? Could it be a coincidence? A shot in the dark? They seemed so persistent when they asked the question – again and again and again: "Did you, or did you not, talk about Egypt and the Arab spring with Hamas?" If they knew about that, did it mean they knew about everything else?

A couple of weeks later I received the letter from the Norwegian National Security Authority stating:

> After a specific and individual overall assessment of the present information in this case, we have concluded that you are not suited for security clearance.

Wanting people to listen,

you can't just tap them on the shoulder anymore.

You have to hit them with a sledgehammer

and then you'll notice

you've got their strict attention

John Doe

INTRODUCTION

WELCOME TO THE DIGITAL ERA OF PALESTINIAN RESISTANCE

It was with the eruption of the Arab Spring that Arab Internet activism in general and hacktivism in particular drew wider attention. By taking down government websites in Tunisia and Bahrain in addition to the Tunisian stock exchange, the Internet was used as a tool for democratic change in the region. Since the Arab Spring we have seen an increase in the ferocity of Arab hacktivist teams with an additional increase in the number of Israeli websites being targeted.

For example, in January 2012 one of the best known cyberattacks against Israel was performed by an Arab hacker, Saudi-based oxOmar, connected to the Saudi Arabian hacker group "group-xp", as they hit the website of the Tel Aviv Stock Exchange and the Israeli El Al Airlines.[1] Although they did not manage to take down the website of the stock exchange itself – only slowing it down considerably – oxOmar had already published 400,000 Israeli credit card numbers the previous week.[2] He simultaneously called for all Muslim hackers to join his online fight against Israel.[3] Seemingly, it opened the eyes of

the Palestinian political specter to hacktivism, as the Palestinian political party Hamas endorsed the call for "electronic jihad", and Hamas'
spokesman, Sami Abu Zuhri, emphasized that the attack opened "a
new arena for resistance against Israeli crimes".[4]

Then-Israeli Deputy Foreign Minister Danny Ayalon vowed
that they would catch the Saudi hackers as the operation was "[a]
breach of sovereignty comparable to a terrorist operation".[5] oxOmar,
on the other hand, did not seem to be too impressed, as he auda-
ciously claimed: "Danny Ayalon proved his stupidity multiple times.
He just talks, 'We'll catch, We'll do, We'll reply, We We We We'll'."[6]

Israel, as usual, did not stand idly by, and shortly after-
wards Israeli hacker teams answered by taking down the websites of
the Saudi Stock Exchange (the Tadāwul) and the Abu Dhabi Securi-
ties Exchange (ADX). Furthermore, the pro-Israeli hacker Hannibal
joined the campaign, publishing the email addresses and Facebook
passwords of Arab nationals.[7] Three months later, in April, oxOmar
died in hospital, 28 years old, after an acute asthma attack due to a
sandstorm hitting Riyadh.[8]

What we witnessed in 2012 was a continuation of cyberattacks on Israel with politico-religious repercussions when, among
others, the Kuwaiti Islamist preacher Tariq Muhammad Suwaydan,
before the attacks on the Israeli flight company El Al Airlines, stated
that Muslims not only had an obligation to conduct political jihad,
but also electronic jihad.[9] Later, after the attacks, he followed up this
notion on Twitter, where he stated: "I see the necessity of uniting the
hackers in the electronic jihad against the Zionist enemy."[10]

Even though these campaigns drew wide media attention, it was not the first time that tensions had risen between the Israeli and Arab cyber-communities. In fact, an Israeli-Arab flare-up in cyber-space can be traced back to around the year 2000 when Israeli hackers crippled the website of Hizbollah by means of Distributed Denial of Service (DDoS) attacks.[11] Since then we have witnessed the emergence of several Palestinian and Arab hacktivist groups such as Gaza Hacker Team, KDMS Team and Anonymous Arab, to mention a few. While most of them have focused their attention on the Israeli websites and cyber-infrastructure, others (for example, KDMS Team) have hacked solely Western ones (such as the websites of the instant-messaging application WhatsApp, AVG anti-virus and the web-analysis company Alexa) to spread awareness about the Palestinian cause.

Little has been written about the phenomenon of Palestinian hacktivism since its emergence, and the same applies to studies of hacktivism as a means of resistance against occupation. Thus, the academic field is underdeveloped, and there will most likely be many years of scholarly research before we can fully understand it. This is an attempt to take that first step.

As I am educated in the field of Arabic and Middle East studies, and not in computer sciences, this is first and foremost a study of the Palestinian resistance and the new means employed in the digital era. Thus, as far as I have been able, I have avoided going too deep into technical issues. Most readers with an interest in hacking and computers are likely to know more about that particular field than I do. Rather, I attempt to answer the following questions: Who are these Palestinian hackers? What are they doing, and why? And last but not least, can hacktivism as it is epitomized by these groups be regarded as a part of the Palestinian resistance against the Israelis?

@ IS FOR ACTIVISM

When the Internet in its modern form first emerged, it was praised as the tool that would not only democratize the business of communication but also enable a free flow of information. For the most optimistic spokespersons of the Internet, it meant the end of exploitation, poverty, militarism, corruption and tyranny.[12] One of the technology-optimists of his time, and mistakenly credited as the inventor of the Internet, Al Gore, went as far as to describe the "information superhighways" as "a metaphor for democracy itself".[13]

However, there are several who point out that the Internet has been subject to the commercialization and logic of capital accumulation and therefore its initial democratic potential has in no way blossomed as was hoped.[14] Edward Snowden's leaks led to the discovery of numerous surveillance programs involving efforts to implement global surveillance, while the second most accessed website in the world, Facebook, is collecting all of our personal information for profit.

As we are using a vast range of different applications and programs in our daily lives, we get the illusion that everything is suddenly for free. The Internet is the all-for-free buffet where we can help ourselves without giving anything back. Yet, as repeated ad nauseam, there is no such thing as a free lunch, and we have come to realize that we are paying with the one commodity we ideally should cherish the most: our privacy. Our sexual, cultural and ideological preferences, our favorite foods and restaurants, and even our movement patterns are being monitored, saved and sold to the highest bidder. It would be an understatement to say that if the utopia has not turned into a dystopia, it has by no means become that which the most optimistic spokespersons envisioned twenty years ago.

Admittedly, it is almost cruel to quote another Internet-optimist, Kevin Kelly, as he presumptuously wrote in 1995: "No one has been more wrong about computerization than George Orwell in *1984*. So far, nearly everything about the actual possibility-space that computers have created indicates they are not the beginning of authority but its end."[15]

This background is important to note, since hacktivism – merging the two words *activism* and *hacking* – was created and shaped in this nodal point between the Internet's democratizing potential and its actual state today. One example is when the first commercial email was sent to all Usenet users in April 1994 and the transmitter was inundated by so many angry emails in reply that the advertiser's inbox shut down. As Robert McChesney, professor at the University of Illinois, points out, the notion among the Usenet users then – which led to this digital form of protest – was that commercialism and Internet democracy could not, and should not, merge.[16]

We have since then witnessed several hacktivist actions/attacks being conducted by different groups. What most of these groups have in common is that they have used hacktivism to promote human rights or to protest against the violation of human rights, disclose confidential information (for example through the use of

WikiLeaks) and prevent the commercialization of the Internet. In other words, we have seen hacktivism as the "marriage of political activism and computer hacking [where] hacktivism combines the transgressive politics of civil disobedience with the technologies and technique of computer hackers".[17]

Although it is hard to put the development of hacking and the emergence of hacktivism into chronological periods, Jordan and Taylor categorize this development in seven stages, with the "original hacker" who experimented with the capabilities of large mainframe computers in the 1950s and 1960s, the "hardware hacker" who played a key role in in the personal computing revolution in the 1970s, and the "software hacker" who changed or created computer programs.[18]

Subsequently, in the mid-1980s we saw the emergence of the "hacker/cracker", who illicitly broke into people's computer systems, and the "microserf" – computer programmers co-opted into the structures of large corporations such as Microsoft.[19]

Then, in the mid-1990s, two streams of hacking emerged which marked "a retreat from ... a pervasive intrusion of commodified values into social life and a concomitant reassertion of more counter-cultural values".[20] First, the "open-source community" re-established the ideal sense of the hack by producing software and developing it through sharing: "Nearly all such software is released free, often with the only licence restriction being that the software cannot be distributed for profit and any improvements must be made available for others to examine and, in turn, improve."[21]

It was precisely in this nodal point between the ideal of Internet democracy and commercialism that we saw the emergence of the hacktivist, whose hacking had a clear political purpose, "whose politics could never be ignored, overlooked or remain hidden in software code. It is the use of computers for direct actions that forms hacktivism as a distinct community within the hacking world".[22]

Although there are several different and conflicting definitions of hacktivism, the one used here is limited to politically and socially motivated hacking. Thus, I exclude the phenomenon of 'Internet activism' where the Internet and especially social media are used politically to mobilize the masses for political causes and demonstrations rather than inflicting direct damage on the target.

It is important to note that hacktivism must not be confused with colorful concepts such as cyber-vandalism, where apparently mischief and sabotage are the only goals and which does nothing more than to infantilize hackers. If we limit ourselves to these definitions, we will lose the ability to analyze the hackers as social and political actors. As Sandor Vegh points out in his doctoral thesis on the Internet's impact on democracy, dismissing hacktivism as cyber-vandalism or cyberterrorism will on the contrary lead to a state where progressives are being pushed, socially and politically, further into the periphery where the Internet is essentially their only opportunity to be heard.[23]

For example, it should be emphasized that cyberterrorism is purely hypothetical, as it has never been done in the history of hacking. Just as there is an academic and popular struggle for the hegemony of defining terrorism, there are necessarily disputing and conflicting narratives where Israel will see any attacks as cyberterrorism, while the Palestinians in most cases will consider it their natural right to resist the occupation.

We have the possibility to conduct different forms of action in the public physical realm, such as sit-in demonstrations, where the goal is to limit the access to public space, and this could be compared to DDoS attacks as it limits access to space in the digital sphere by overwhelming a server with so many requests that a website goes down for a limited period of time.

It is like pouring water down a funnel. If you have several glasses of water and pour them down one by one, everything will be fine. But if you pour down all the water at once, it will inevitably flow over because the funnel cannot handle the volume. The same applies for DDoS attacks when thousands of computers are sending so many requests simultaneously that the server cannot handle them all.

That is not to say that DDoS attacks are not controversial, and their use as a means to influence political and social change is disputed, including in the hacker environment. The hacker Oxblood Ruffin from the Cult of the Dead Cow (cDc), formed back in 1984, distanced himself from it as it was something which limits free speech and the free flow of information: "Denial of Service attacks are a violation of the First Amendment, and the freedom of expression and assembly. No rationale, even in the service of the highest ideals, makes them anything other than what they are – illegal, unethical, and uncivil."[24]

Furthermore, John Perry Barlow, founding member of the digital rights group Electronic Frontier Foundation, expressed his opposition as: "I support freedom of expression, no matter whose, so I oppose DDoS attacks regardless of their target ... They're poison gas of cyberspace."[25]

Yet their argument is somewhat flawed. DDoS attacks are not the same as taking down a website or a forum permanently – which I also consider somewhat problematic – but rather for a shorter period of time, where the goal is in fact to influence the public agenda. If the goal of a sit-in demonstration in front of a parliament was to hinder the politicians' access to it permanently, it would contain a qualitatively different political character than if it was to do so for a couple of hours to protest against the war in Iraq.

Is it an effective means? Perhaps. Is it undemocratic? Certainly not.

Furthermore, hackers "defacing" a website by changing its visual content – using text, pictures, videos and sound to present a message – can be compared to graffiti in the public physical realm. Just as not all graffiti can be considered political, as some of it is in fact limited to vandalism, a defacement that does nothing more than to "tag" a website would also fall outside the definition of hacktivism.

Jordan and Taylor point out that since the emergence of popular political movements there have been protests, demonstrations, boycotts and other means to obtain a certain goal in the physical realm. Thus:

> Hacktivism attempts to translate the principles of direct action into virtuality. The sit-in or blockade that occurs in the streets and aims to cause a meeting to fail, can be matched by a blockade of online messages, which aims to make computer support for the meeting to fail.[26]

9

Therefore, we should approach the phenomenon of hacktivism as a new kind of political protest that is historically conditioned: protests during the digitalization of political pressure. Just as traditional political groups or parties were, and still are, publishing communiqués, leaflets or newspapers, hacktivists are using Twitter and Facebook accounts, personal websites/homepages, to mention a few, in order to promote their cause. Hacking is today so mainstream that we now have hackers with their own podcasts and hacker conventions.[27]

If this narrative of hacktivism is the foundation, it means that there are direct links from Palestinian activists arranging a sit-in demonstration in protest against the occupation, to today's Palestinian *hack*tivists doing the same thing in the digital sphere. As we in the physical realm have activism (awareness campaigns and boycotts), political civil disobedience (sit-ins and demonstrations) and legitimate and illegitimate armed resistance (attacks on Israeli soldiers, settlers and civilians), so do we have Internet activism (online petition campaigns), the already mentioned digital civil disobedience and cyberterrorism (for example, hijacking airplanes by hacking their control systems).

PART I

HEADING FOR THE
MILITARY–DIGITAL COMPLEX

1

THE RESISTANCE DEVELOPS

Palestinian hacktivism and electronic jihad cannot be seen in isolation from the Palestinian resistance movement itself. Instead, it should be considered as the digitalization and development of an already existing resistance – based on the necessities and challenges facing people under a persisting military-technological occupation.

Of course, to define "resistance" is not a simple task. Not only because the term contains qualitatively different means and strategies such as armed/non-violent and active/passive resistance, but also because the term is politically charged. That is, politically charged as far as it implies legality, contrary to the term "terrorism", which implies illegality. Also, the Palestinian resistance movement's approach to a future statehood and the means to achieve it has been historically conditioned and oriented according to what the Palestinians themselves have regarded as possible. Thus, the resistance and its goals have changed several times throughout its history.

We should not get trapped by the normalizing narrative of a conflict between "equals", a conflict where Israelis and Palestinians are simply two neighbors who just cannot seem to get along. It is first and foremost expressed through one of the words which, perhaps, appears most frequently in this book: "occupation". Israel not only disputes the notion of the illegality of the occupation but also that an occupation even exists. However, international law, despite its at times obvious flaws, has to be applied to any ongoing conflict. Thus, when using the term occupation, I am referring to UN resolution 242 declaring the occupation of the Palestinian territories to be illegal and that the Israeli army must be withdrawn immediately, and to UN resolution 194, which states the Palestinian refugees' right of return. These are undisputable human rights.

Last, I also refer to the International Court of Justice (ICJ) deeming the wall and settlements as illegal and in breach of international law. Thus, as a professor at the University of Oslo emphasized in a seminar: "No doubt one has to be objective, but if you point out that Israel is breaking international law, you are not being subjective – you are referring to an objective fact." So when I refer to the Palestinian resistance, I am referring to a people's use of violent and non-violent means to end or change a particular kind of political situation such as an occupation. The term "occupation" also denotes an objective reality: that is, the ensuing rights of the Palestinians within that context – including the right to resist. It is precisely this resistance that has developed according to the local and global situation, with the associated challenges that the resistance has faced. From the Cold War to the fall of the Berlin Wall; from the Oslo process to the "War on Terror".

Of course, the goals of the Palestinian resistance have not been limited to directly forcing Israel to end its occupation, but also aim to make the international community aware that there actually is such a thing as a Palestinian people with a lost home.

When we analyze this resistance, it must be based on the notion that human beings, and our way of organizing, are historical products formed by the contradictions of society at large and within the resistance movement itself. This means that the issues raised and the strategies proposed by the Palestinian resistance through different periods of time are not historical abstracts. Ellen Meiksins Wood's assessment of Western political thought may be useful:

> To understand what political theorists are saying requires
> knowing what questions they are trying to answer, and
> those questions confront them not simply as philosophical
> abstractions but as specific historical conditions, in the context
> of specific practical activities, social relations, pressing issues,
> grievances and conflict.[1]

Thus, the account of the history of the Palestinian resistance is by virtue an account of a social history. My intent here is not to give the reader a full account of Palestinian history. Rather, I wish to present a glimpse of the wider and longer threads that run through it in order to understand how Palestinian hacktivism fits in as a continuation: From the fidā'ī and symbolic violence, the shahīd and non-violence, and subsequently the istishhādī and emergence of electronic jihad.

THE FIDĀʾĪ: "I WILL DIE AS A WARRIOR – UNTIL MY COUNTRY RETURNS"

Before the establishment of Israel in 1948 – through what several Israeli historians, such as Ilan Pappé and Benny Morris, have argued to be the ethnic cleansing of the Palestinians[2] – the region had already seen organized protests and campaigns against the colonization of the homeland through boycotts, demonstrations, armed resistance, general strikes and graffiti to name a few. However, in 1955 – following a period of shock and apathy after the *nakba* (the catastrophe) – the Palestinian refugees began to organize themselves in commando units.[3] It was the beginning of a new era of resistance and military campaigns against the Israeli state – in which the only perceived way of liberating Palestine was through armed means.

The armed campaigns were mainly small-scale attacks conducted from Gaza, Lebanon, Syria and Jordan against Israeli military sites and settlements – also called pinprick guerilla tactics, given the name from the small hole made by a needle – used by the Palestinian resistance in order to frustrate and exhaust a superior Israeli army, and also sometimes inciting excessive reprisals.

As many of the operations resulted in the death of the fighter, they were branded as fidāʾiyyīn (the ones who sacrifice themselves). The campaigns of the fidāʾī were, however, not limited to pure military campaigns but contained within them the notion of ṣumūd (steadfastness). For example, the fidāʾī would in many cases harvest the crops of their former farms and retrieve their livestock.

During this time the Palestinian resistance created several cultural perceptions, with the fidāʾī as a cultural icon, the klashīn (the Kalashnikov) as a symbol of pride and the Palestinian songs of "revolution, resistance, sacrifice, return and self-reliance".[4] There was thus a consistent secular-nationalist notion in the narrative of the fidāʾī in accordance with the prevailing ideology of that time, secular Arab socialism/pan-Arabism.

It should be mentioned that the fidāʾī who died in battle would still be considered a martyr, yet, as the Palestinian-American anthropologist Nasser Abufarha points out, although the military campaigns to a large extent were an act of sacrifice, that did not necessarily include a religious dimension as it would later on.[5] Rather, "In the Palestinian context the perception of fusion between the human sacrificer and the land is more prevalent than fusion with divine life, especially in cultural representations, although the latter also exists".[6]

Nevertheless, although they faced a superior opponent in the Israeli state, it is hard to underestimate the sheer optimism in the narrative of the fidāʾī, where a future victory and the liberation of Palestine seemed inevitable. Partly, the optimism of the fidāʾī was linked to the fact that the liberation of Palestine through armed means was not something limited to the Palestinian cause, but rather a phenomenon in the global development of decolonization. This period of time saw the armed struggle against colonialism in Vietnam (1955–1975) and in Algeria (1954–1962), to mention just two, and in the majority of cases the former colonies achieved independence. The Palestinian resistance studied these different armed anti-colonial movements in detail. They were the embodiment of Frantz Fanon's thesis: "Decolonization is the veritable creation of new men. But this creation owes nothing of its legitimacy to any supernatural power; the 'thing' which has been colonized becomes man during the same process by which it frees itself."[7]

This is not to say that the campaigns of the Palestine Liberation Organization (PLO) and its fidā'iyyīn were perfect. On the contrary, the movement managed to get into conflict, first with King Hussein of Jordan as in the beginning he resisted the idea of the PLO establishing itself in Jordanian-occupied East Jerusalem, and feared that the Palestinians would later on attempt to overthrow him and take over Palestine.[8] Later, in 1964, he would accept the claim after pressure from Nasser.

The March 1968 victory at Karameh in Jordan, then headquarters of the PLO's dominant faction, Fatah, where the Palestinians, with decisive aid from the Jordanian military, managed to fight off 15,000 Israeli soldiers, and further entrenched its legitimacy, did not help. For example, as a result of Karameh, the Palestinian organizations strengthened their positions in the Palestinian refugee camps and members of Fatah and the Marxist-Leninist Popular Front for the Liberation of Palestine (PFLP) established themselves in the camps of Wihdat, Baqa'a, Sulh, al-Husn, Jerash, Zizia in the north and outside of Tufila, Shubaq and Karak in the south.[9] Subsequently, there were several clashes between the Palestinians and Jordanians, and in November that same year, three of the PFLP's training camps were bombed by the Jordanian monarchy.[10]

It all culminated two years later in 1970, in what would be known as Black September. First, the Palestinian guerillas attempted to assassinate King Hussein, an attack which he barely survived, and then the PFLP hijacked three airplanes that were forced to land in Jordan; shortly after Yasser Arafat declared Irbid District of Jordan a liberated zone.[11] If decolonization creates new men, there is apparently no guarantee that the same men will not be overcome by bravado. The repercussions of Black September, which lasted from September 1970 until July 1971, led to the loss of thousands of Palestinian lives.

As the Palestinian resistance was expelled from Jordan and moved to Lebanon, the "pinprick" operations of the fidā'ī decreased. However, the tactics and the establishment of fidā'ī bases in their new host country created tensions with the Lebanese population, which started to consider the PLO and the rest of the Palestinian resistance as a threat to the stability of the country. The fact that the majority of Palestinians are Sunni Muslims and Lebanon had, and still has, a principle of power distribution along religious and sectarian lines did not make it any easier. In 1982, as a result of the war in Lebanon, the PLO – humiliated and disarmed – moved to Tunisia, where it would remain irrelevant for a decade. The final sacrifice of the fidā'ī had been made.

COUNTERING THE SYMBOLIC VIOLENCE

In retrospect, it is important to keep in mind that the goals of the Palestinian resistance were not limited to the military defeat of Israel. We should not forget that the aftermath of the *nakba* happened in a period when a majority of the Western world held deep sympathies for the Israeli state project because of the Holocaust. Furthermore, there were not that many people who even knew such a thing as the

Palestinian people existed. While the majority today is sympathetic to the Palestinian cause, it would have been unthinkable to question the legitimacy of Israel in the 1950s, 1960s, and even into the 1970s.

The myth that the Jews had come to the land and made the desert bloom was prevalent, with the corresponding idea that the "lazy" Arabs only came later on to reap the benefits. Yet, as a Polish rabbi reported coming back from Palestine in 1920, "The bride is beautiful, but she has got a bridegroom already".[12] Fortunately for the Zionists, as Golda Meir expressed it, "I thank God every night that the bridegroom was so weak, and the bride could be taken away from him".[13] Simply put, it was a period when it was not controversial to claim that "There is no such thing as a Palestinian people ... They didn't exist", as was done by the same Israeli prime minister, Golda Meir.[14] The Palestinians thus saw the necessity to create their own existence as if they were a child forced to give birth to itself. For them, the saying "To resist is to exist" was not just a meaningless phrase.

It is only within this context that we can understand what happened. In 1970 parts of the resistance – predominantly through the Marxist-Leninist PFLP – started hijacking international flights. As George Habash, then leader of the PFLP, stated: "When we hijack a plane it has more effect than if we killed a hundred Israelis in battle", and "For decades, world public opinion has been neither for nor against the Palestinians. It simply ignored us. At least the world is talking about us now."[15]

Thus, the Palestinian armed resistance was not limited to imposing direct damage on the Israeli state, but aimed to enhance its symbolic power where none existed. One can say that the Palestinian resistance emerged not only as a result of the objective violence of bullets and bombs but also from the imposition of the symbolic violence associated with the production of knowledge in the Israeli/Palestinian conflict. The hijacking of airplanes was not a mere act of what Slavoj Žižek terms "visible 'subjective' violence", that is "the perturbation of the 'normal' peaceful state of things".[16] Rather, it was an act of counter-symbolic violence resulting from the actual situation of that time and the hopes for tomorrow.

Indeed, we could moralize as if the unfolding events were created in a political void; but instead, perhaps we should remember the German officer who visited Picasso in his Paris studio during the Second World War. When he saw the painting *Guernica*, depicting the German bombing of the Basque city, he asked Picasso, shocked: "Did you do this?" Calmly Picasso replied: "No, *you* did this!"[17]

2

THE SHAHĪD AND THE
NORMALIZATION OF OCCUPATION

While the PLO and the rest of the Palestinian resistance had emerged in a time of decolonization, in the 1980s the global situation had changed drastically. Decolonization and armed struggle for liberation had to large degree ended – and with the fall of the Berlin Wall the Cold War did too. In other words, what had been seen as the Great War of Ideologies, capitalism versus communism, had come to an end with what Francis Fukuyama termed "the end of history".[1] Capitalism and its hegemony had won and what awaited was for the rest of the world to adopt that notion. It was in this period, after the defeat of the PLO in Lebanon in 1982 and while the traditional Palestinian resistance faced a situation of irrelevance and isolation in Tunisia, that two new currents emerged.

First, a new generation of Palestinians emerged in the Palestinian territories and with it new leaders who were growing restless after twenty years of a seemingly unending occupation of the Palestinian territories.[2] Hence, the resistance moved its geographical center from the Arab countries neighboring Israel to the occupied territories themselves for the first time since 1948.

Second, the defeat of the PLO, not merely as a resistance movement but also as a secular movement, led to the rise of the Islamic resistance and its religious superstructure through movements such as Hamas (the former Palestinian wing of the Muslim Brotherhood) and Palestinian Islamic Jihad. Although the use of religion in the resistance was growing with these movements as they appropriated larger parts of the *definitionsmacht* – the power to define the social, cultural and moral reality – it should be emphasized that they were still nationalist in their goals and programs.

On the other hand, the rise of the Islamic political movements cannot be seen as a strictly Palestinian phenomenon, but rather was a broader regional development. As the defeat of Gamal Abdel Nasser in the Six Day War in 1967 represented the end of secular pan-Arabism, the Islamic revolution in Iran, in 1979, was by many perceived as the success of political Islam in imposing real change and restoring dignity for the Arab and Muslim masses. This led to new currents not only in Palestine with Hamas, but also in, for example, Lebanon with the rise of Hizbollah in 1985.

With the outbreak of the First Intifada in late 1987, the Palestinian resistance changed its discourse, rhetoric and tactics. One example is the growing notion that it was necessary to create international pressure on Israel in order to make it withdraw from the occupied territories. Another was the emerging religious superstructure of the resistance in line with the increasing impact of the Islamist Palestinian parties and movements: From the secular fidāʾī who acted as an active subject by his autonomous action of "sacrificing himself" and merging his body with the land, the resistance moved to the Palestinian shahīd (martyr) who, as a passive object, was killed by forces external to him within the framework of a distinct religious dimension.[3] In this case Palestinians were martyred by a superior and oppressive military army for the relatively harmless action of, for example, throwing rocks against a tank. And thus the notion of the shahīd was the transcendence of the initial victimization to that of becoming a national hero.

During the First Intifada, through pictures of youths throwing rocks, boycotts and general strikes that were brutally repressed by the Israeli forces, the pressure on Israel from international society and from within mounted. As mentioned, the shahīd was not merely a Palestinian national hero and symbol, but someone transcending the identity and status of a victim that the world could not ignore. After all, Yitzhak Rabin, who at that time was the Israeli defense minister, was referred to as the "bone-breaker",[4] a name he acquired after ordering Israeli soldiers to break the arms and legs of Palestinian children throwing stones.

The change from the fidā'ī to the shahīd also embodies the change of a resistance movement and a people: from initially believing in the possibility of liberating themselves through armed means, to focusing on the international community as the best medium to impose a solution.

However, this is not to say that the armed Palestinian resistance was on its death bed. Rather, a change happened, where the traditional Palestinian resistance, mainly represented by the parties in the PLO, rejected armed means while the Islamist parties took up the baton. For example, in its opposition to the Oslo Accords – the start of the peace process between the PLO and Israel, and seen by some Palestinians as a betrayal of the Palestinian cause – Hamas launched its first suicide bomb attack in the West Bank in 1993.[5] Later, Hamas would continue with suicide bombings after the massacre committed by the Israeli settler Baruch Goldstein in Hebron in 1994.[6]

Yet a qualification is necessary. The Palestinian resistance was never unified in its goal, tactics and ideology, and the split which emerged between the Islamist movements that rejected the Oslo Accords and those submitting to the negotiations was a continuation from 1974. Namely, the Rejectionist Front (Jabhat al-Rafaḍ) consisting of, among others, the DFLP (Democratic Front for the Liberation of Palestine), PFLP (Popular Front for the Liberation of Palestine), PLFP General Command and Abū Niḍāl's Fatah Revolutionary Council, which rejected the PLO's Ten Point Program – a program that implied only a partial liberation of Palestine with the possibility of using only non-violent means. Thus, the split in the resistance movement during the Oslo Accords was a continuation of the disagreement over the benefits and disadvantages of armed resistance versus negotiations and recognition of the state of Israel.

These contradictions and the additional rivalry between the factions would later lead to catastrophe.

THE PALESTINIAN NON-VIOLENT RESISTANCE

So far, it would seem that the Palestinian resistance was only limited to the armed struggle; however, the majority of the resistance has in fact historically been non-violent, similar to the US civil rights movement. This is the resistance that the majority of Palestinians are conducting every single day – either passively or actively.

The embodiment of the First Intifada was first and foremost civil disobedience and grassroots resistance through general strikes, boycotts, graffiti and throwing stones. Yet these campaigns were dependent on the committees, *al-lajin*, which coordinated, mobilized and orchestrated the popular action in order to break the Israeli occupation.[7] More importantly, in contrast to the Second Intifada seven years later, the Palestinians were united for a common cause – it was in its essence revolutionary since it was organized for and by the Palestinian people, independently from the leaders in Tunis talking on their behalf. Also, the participation in these committees, organizations and clubs introduced and familiarized groups of Palestinians with political processes and group decision making.[8] The committees were the means to the transformation of a people in itself into a people for itself.

When the pictures of the resistance arrived on the desks of the international news agencies, it was the Palestinian child throwing stones at Israeli tanks that dominated the discourse. As the cliché goes, it was the modern version of David and Goliath – the small child slinging a stone against the mighty giant. This is not to say that the stone-throwing children necessarily were political cadres who saw their actions as a means to transcend victimization, but rather acted out of frustration and anger. As the Israeli journalist Amira Hass described it: "It is the adjective attached to the subject of 'We've had enough of you, occupiers'."[9]

In their account of the history of Palestinian popular resistance Darweish and Rigby have summarized the activism and resistance of the First Intifada as *symbolic, polemical, offensive, defensive* and *constructive* resistance. The two former entailed changing the time on their clocks from Israeli to Palestinian time, by changing between summer- and wintertime one week ahead, in addition to undermining Israeli authority and conducting the aforementioned boycotts. The offensive and the defensive resistance entailed direct confrontations with Israeli soldiers (for example stone-throwing) and the support, protection and medical help enabling them to do so. The defensive resistance, and the least visible of these forms of resistance, was the result of the economic hardship the Palestinians were suffering as a result of the strikes and lack of income, where they promoted new forms of home-based incomes.[10]

It is nevertheless disputed whether stone-throwing can be seen as non-violent. But perhaps that is a minor digression and also a misunderstanding, since non-violence is often considered synonymous with pacifism. While the latter is an absolutist moral position which rejects any form of violence or aggressive means, stone-throwing is situated somewhere in between; pacifism is, for example, not a moral end in itself. What divides supporters of non-violence from pacifists is that violence can be used to prevent even greater suffering. If, for the sake of argument, we should then declare stone-throwing violent, it is not the same as declaring it immoral. This contradiction is beautifully captured in the statement of a Palestinian activist from Walajah: "Stone throwing is violent but it is a part of the popular resistance. We call it popular resistance, not peaceful resistance, so it includes stone throwing."[11]

Last but not least, the concept of ṣumūd (steadfastness), which runs back to the beginning of the colonization itself, should be noted. As the Palestinians share an experience of dispossession, colonization and subjugation, their fear has not only been related to the destruction of their property and their human rights, but has also extended to fear for their actual identity.[12] Thus, for the Palestinians, their existence in itself became a form of resistance, often with the Palestinian peasant as a symbol; where those olive trees uprooted by the occupiers would be continuously replanted by him in order for his children to be able to inherit his land.[13]

It has been branded as a form of passive resistance, and, admittedly, so it was during the glorification of the armed struggle in the age of the fidā'ī, when the Palestinians of the occupied territories were asked to stay steadfast and wait for liberation by the PLO.[14] Yet ṣumūd, a form of symbolic resistance, does entail a type of agency by virtue of the constructive resistance it requires and necessarily produces. For example, for it to be possible, Palestinians in solidarity with each other would collect supplies essential for life, such as food – necessary as the dispossessed received virtually no support from the UN or any other international agency – which created a sense of "communal solidarity".[15]

As ṣumūd was the blood flowing through the veins of the Palestinian resistance in the occupied territories, the Palestinians did simultaneously change the essence of their celebrations and ceremonies into resistance, where "Weddings, national and religious celebrations became a medium for political expression and singing national songs as a quiet way of challenging military rule".[16] Thus, in their passive form of resistance they were transcending the initial meaning of an act which usually is perceived as essentially *a*political. It might not seem the greatest threat to the Israeli occupation, but such expressions were the glue of the social fabric of the Palestinian community ("communal solidarity") necessary to cope with the situation.

As Bertolt Brecht, in the centerpiece of the poem "Legend of the Origin of the *Book of Tao-tê-ching* on Lao-Tsû's Road into Exile", reflects on the paradox of action and non-action: "He learnt how quite soft water, by attrition / Over the years will grind strong rocks away. / In other words, that hardness must lose the day."[17]

3

A DIGITAL FORTRESS: THE ISRAELI MILITARY–DIGITAL COMPLEX

In the whole period described above, the world had experienced a technological revolution with the introduction of the Internet. As most of the literature on the topic describes its impact in the West, it might be wise to dwell briefly on the development in the Arab world in general, and in Israel and Palestine specifically, before returning to the development of the Palestinian resistance in the next chapter.

Although the Internet was introduced in Tunisia in 1991 with its NSFNET connection – and then in Kuwait, Egypt and the United Arab Emirates in the following two years – the development of the Arab cyber-infrastructure was initially slow and comparatively delayed. Saudi Arabia, Libya and Iraq were, for example, the last to introduce it for the public in 1999, 2001 and with mass access to the Internet as late as 2003 for Iraq. One of many reasons for the initially slow development was the fact that many autocratic leaders considered Internet access as a threat to their rule, a threat to a moral/pious life and as an obfuscator of traditional social borders between genders.

It is, however, important to emphasize that the degree of censorship varies between the different Arab countries depending on rule, traditions, development of infrastructure and degree of religious/ moral conservatism. After all, there is still no such thing as a monolithic "Arab" system for the whole Middle East and North Africa, or some kind of *homo islamicus.*

In 2014, Saudi Arabia, Yemen and Syria were the Arab countries coming out worst in terms of Internet censorship, with the banning of both morally and politically "inappropriate" content. On the other hand, Jordan, Morocco, Sudan and Kuwait are rather more liberal, with restrictions on pornographic content, selected political media and torrents. Iraq, Egypt, Algeria, Lebanon and Israel only have restrictions on the latter while Bahrain, Oman, Tunisia, the Gaza Strip (Palestine), Qatar and the United Arab Emirates restrict access to pornography. Although there is no detailed description of Libya in the overview, its level of Internet censorship is labeled as "medium restriction level".[1] With the chaos raging in the country after "democracy" arrived, it would be safe to assume that Internet censorship is not high on the agenda.

Also, the means of keeping control over the Arab populations varies. In Sudan the Internet was, on the one hand, only introduced and allowed in 1997/1998 with "Sudanet" as the only Internet Service Provider (ISP) at the time, and with the Sudanese security service having full access to all traffic.[2] In contrast, the more lenient but nevertheless repressive Egypt established the Department to Combat Crimes of Computers and Internet in 2004 in order to crack down on "subversive" websites.[3]

Yet it should be pointed out that the slow rate of Internet growth cannot simply be attributed to the repressive regimes in the region. It also has to do with technological limitations. For example, during the 1990s only Roman scripts were available, and the first Arabic language email was not launched until 2000 by Maktoob. The social media platform Facebook did not add an Arabic-language interface until 2009. Although the Arabic-language content has grown and is more widely available, there are still problems: for example, searches in Arabic often deliver random results and lead to "a forum rather than a well-designed website".[4]

Poverty also matters. With an initially high cost for Arabic ISPs, and a generally low level of income, there have been few possibilities for the Arab population – limiting access to the few in the upper middle class and bourgeoisie. Although some argue that literacy levels play a role in the subnormal speed of cyber-development in the Arab world, as Peter Vincent and Barney Warf do,[5] that does not explain how the United Arab Emirates, Qatar, Kuwait and Bahrain, which are the top four countries in terms of Internet penetration, fail to be in the same positions when it comes to the literacy rate. As Deborah L. Wheeler points out, the four Arab countries with the highest literacy rate, Palestine, Jordan, Lebanon and Libya, rank eleventh, seventh, fifth and fifteenth in terms of Internet penetration.[6] However, we should not dichotomize these two positions as they do not necessarily oppose each other, since the economic and educational factors intersect and overlap one another.

This does not mean that the development of the Internet in the Arab world has stagnated. On the contrary, in 2006 the Internet in the Arab world was growing at a higher rate than any other place on earth,[7] but in the period 2009–2013 it was surpassed by Africa in Internet penetration of households, with an "annual growth of 27%, followed by 15% annual growth in Asia and the Pacific, the Arab States and the CIS".[8] Furthermore, the United Arab Emirates has introduced the younger generations to information technology and computing at an early stage, seeing IT as the means to economic progress,[9] while Hosni Mubarak attempted to create an IT revolution in Egypt.[10]

THE ARAB SPRING AND TWITTER REVOLUTIONS

In other words, despite its initial limitations the Internet has made its mark on Arab society. For example, the Internet has enabled interaction with the opposite sex through chat rooms, Facebook, Twitter and other forms of social media. The opportunity afforded by blogs has also created a new genre within Arabic literature, so-called "blog literature" ('adab al-mudawanna), with Rajaa al-Sanea's novel *Girls of Riyadh* (2007) as an example. Some even went as far as to call the revolutions in Tunisia and Egypt a "Twitter" and "Facebook revolution", giving credit to social media for their success. This notion is most persistent among activists and journalists, such as the Egyptian-American journalist Mona Eltahawy, but is also present in academic circles.[11]

If we look at the Internet in the Arab world strictly in the context of Arab hacktivism, we have seen cases in both Tunisia and Egypt – depending on a broad or narrow definition of the term. For example, during the revolution in Tunisia several government websites were hacked and the website of the Tunisian stock exchange was brought down – placing the event within the mainstream definition of hacktivism. By the broad definition of hacktivism, Arab hacktivism also includes Egypt, where activists on the streets used proxy servers to circumvent website blocking, continue mobilizing for demonstrations and sharing information about the ongoing events with the rest of the world – as narrated by Wael Ghonim in the book *Revolution 2.0: The Power of the People is Stronger than the People in Power* (2012).

It should be emphasized that there is an ongoing debate between so-called cyber-skeptics and cyber-optimists whether the overthrow of Hosni Mubarak in Egypt and Zine al-Abidine Ben Ali in Tunisia was a direct result of the use of social media and the impact of the Internet. However, research on the role social media played in shaping the way Egyptians learned about the protests, and the way it influenced them planning their involvement, shows that we need a more nuanced understanding of the events.

Zeynep Tufekci and Christopher Wilson come up with an important correction to the enthusiasts of the so-called Twitter revolution when they state that we cannot limit our perception of the "connectivity infrastructure" to a specific platform or device. We must rather render it as a complex ecology where TV channels (the conveyor of events), social media such as Twitter and Facebook, and the increased access to mobile phones ease both access to and the ability to play the role of an agent or a promoter.[12]

It is, in other words, inaccurate to say that it was Facebook and Twitter which caused and led the revolutions to success as if it were the online petitions, the discussion forums and Facebook pages that were the straw that broke the camel's back. Social media *did* play a role, but rather as a means to spread news, information and support, functioning as much-needed fertilizer for the ongoing demonstrations.[13]

Nevertheless, the role of the Internet during the revolutions aside, it is possible to argue that the Internet in the Arab world has enhanced access to not just information but also a space for discussion and exchange of ideas and thus it also creates a space to question religious leaders, leaders of the state and other authorities. As Wheeler argues: "Internet experimentation can help to foster a political consciousness; boundary transgressions which can bring citizens into deliberations with people beyond their normal social networks, and acquisitions of knowledge and experience."[14]

Then again, the joke goes: if someone arrived from fifty years in the past, the hardest thing to explain to them is that we have a tool that gives us all the information in the whole world, yet the majority of the time is spent looking at pictures of cats and getting into arguments with strangers.

And there is sadly some truth to it. As Belarusian Evgeny Morozov deconstructs the myth that the Internet inevitably will lead to politically aware masses interacting in some kind of Habermasian deliberation, and becoming prone to revolution, he points out that, in fact, pornography, instant-messaging and email "still occupies proportionally much more space than politics and news".[15]

Furthermore, what most young adults do on the Internet revolves around talking to each other or downloading entertainment. The Internet has not become the tool enabling revolution but its opposite; the opium of the masses, not activating but pacifying them. Although the Arab Spring developed into an almost Badiouan event,[16] as it opened up a space with its rupture of the perception of "normality", Morozov shows the flipside of the Twitter utopia narrative:

> There are a lot of dangers and fears we do not entirely understand at this point. What we don't realize is that Twitter, despite all its virtues is actually a public platform. If you do want to plan a revolution on Twitter, you know, your actions will be visible to everyone. In the past, states used to torture to get this kind of data; I mean, now all you have to do is get on Facebook.[17]

THE MILITARIZED ISRAELI HIGH-TECH STATE

The development of the Internet in Palestine has, on the other hand, been different from its development in the rest of the Arab world. This can mainly be explained by the inextricably close connection to Israel since – without any state power and/or monopoly for the Palestinians – the Israelis have had full control over the infrastructure in the Palestinian territories, including telephone lines. Thus, the development of a cyber-infrastructure in the Palestinian territories has been closely connected to its development in Israel, mainly the Israeli transition from the military-industrial to the military–digital complex, and the Israeli high-tech sector's close links to the Israeli military.

As Israel acquired its first commercial ISP in 1992, only slightly before most of the other countries in the Middle East, there appear to be great similarities in the development of the Internet in Israel and the rest of the region. Yet Israel has today grown to be one of the leading producers of high-tech components and products. The country has done so to such an extent that the cluster of companies developing and producing information and communications technology (ICT) in the Tel Aviv area has been branded Silicon Wadi (*wādī* meaning valley in both Arabic and Hebrew) – second only to the original Silicon Valley in California.[18] However, to understand the development of the ICT industry in Israel, one has to look at its close links with the Israeli military and its connection to the Israeli occupation of the Palestinian territories.

When the American President Dwight D. Eisenhower resigned from office in 1961, he warned against a new development in the American economy which he termed the "military-industrial complex", a development of growing influence on US policy as a result of the merging of interests between the US military and commercial industries.[19] Eisenhower's warning against the military-industrial complex, and its development into what would later be known as the military–digital complex, could have been made to Israel: as Israel from the beginning needed to control a vast human population – the Palestinians – and felt the threat from the surrounding Arab states, the military played a major role in the forming of Israeli society. This was both in terms of the enrollment of a large number of Israelis into the army and the large amount of money that was spent on the military industry.

This specifically reflected on its economy in times of unrest, such as after the wars in 1967 and 1973, and the Israeli occupation following the 1967 Six Day War, when Israeli defense spending surged.[20] For example, in 1956, the year of the Suez crisis, 50 percent of the national budget was used to cover military expenses. Subsequently, military expenditures constituted 9.9 percent of Israel's GDP in 1966, 29 percent in 1973, 30.3 percent in 1975, and in the period 1976–1984 military expenditures constituted 24.7 percent of GDP.[21] Thus, in the period 1955–1975 overall Israeli military expenditures had grown staggering twenty times;[22] in 1970 the Israeli arms industry accounted for 10 percent of Israel's overall exports, and 10 percent of the country's population worked in the national arms industry.[23] This inevitably affected the economy, in which arms production was termed the "core of industry".[24]

One clear example is how, when the defense burden started to rise in the late 1960s, investment simultaneously declined, and the unilateral focus on the military caused a fall in Israeli GDP per capita from an annual average of 9.9 percent in the period 1967–1972, to 0.8 percent from 1973 to 1976.[25]

Defense spending's impact on Israeli economic growth had to be altered, and with the forced liberalization of the Israeli economy in the 1980s, there was a move from the low-technology base toward the development of a high-tech industry. Consequently, "In 2001, 80 percent of industrial exports came from the high-tech sector",[26] and "Israel has become the world's No. 2 exporter of cyber products and services after the US".[27] As defense budgets were reduced in the 1980s, so investment began to rise again, to the level before 1967.[28]

The shift was obviously not only a result of ideological currents but also of the end of the Cold War, which led to a "collapse"

Figure 3.1. Defense expenditures 1955–1977, billion NIS (2010 prices)

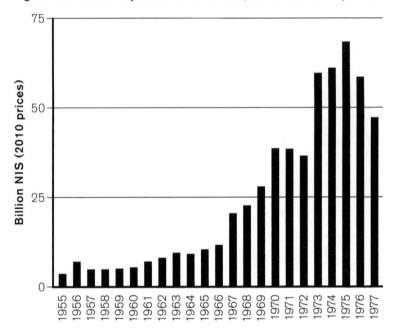

Source: State of Israel (2014) *Defense Expenditures in Israel 1950–2012*.
Note: Figure taken from Lysestøl, P. M. (2016) *Israel Bak Muren av Myter og Propaganda*. Oslo: Forlaget Manifest, p. 108. Reprinted with the permission of the author who has the rights.

of the global arms market, due to the end of the arms race between the US and the Soviet Union. With the subsequent "decline in profitability suffered by the military-industrial sector",[29] military purchases were curtailed in every sense possible at the same time as military exports declined significantly.[30]

However, that was in 1995. Many did believe the end of the Cold War was the actual "end of history", with the victory of liberal democracy, as Francis Fukuyama proclaimed, and so was the case with the Oslo process.[31] Why would you then need a big arms industry? Yet things change at a fast pace and twenty years later, with the "War on Terror", Israeli arms production is surging.

What makes Israeli high-tech production so confusing is that there is no clear-cut line between military and civilian applications. This is epitomized on the website of the Israel Export and International Cooperation Institute where it is promoted on the issue of homeland security: "a direct *military need* with a *high-tech edge*".[32] It is, as Jeff Halper explains, a "[c]ombination of innovative high-tech with a readiness to provide services to any customer and in a technical manner that ignores or minimizes individual privacy or human rights … in which 'security' trumps all else".[33]

This shift to an Israeli high-tech and ICT industry was only made possible by several enabling factors. Whereas several countries had avoided investments in Israel because of regional instability (at least officially), the circumstances changed after the 1993 Oslo Accords when the Israeli government sought to make the economy as "company-friendly" as possible. For example, whereas Intel – one of the world's largest producers of microchips – had to pay over 30 percent of its income in taxes in the US, the taxes in Israel were almost zero.[34] Furthermore, to illustrate the situation in Israel for high-tech companies, in 1996, when Israel had the largest deficit of all the OECD countries, it still chose to subsidize Intel by $900 million in order to persuade it to invest in the country. In 2012, Intel would account for 10 percent of Israel's industrial exports.[35]

This period saw a "tidal wave", where foreign money, in terms of investment and buying local Israeli high-technology

Figure 3.2: Gross expenditures on research and development (percentage of GDP)

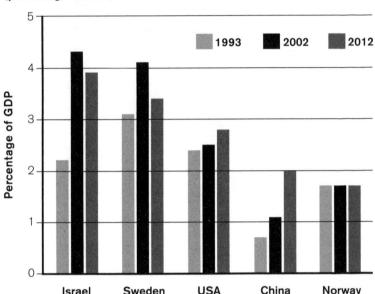

Source: OECD, "Gross domestic spending on R&D", https://data.oecd.org/chart/4vtx

Note: Figure taken from Lysestøl, P. M. (2016) *Israel Bak Muren av Myter og Propaganda*. Oslo: Forlaget Manifest, p. 130. Reprinted with the permission of the author who has the rights.

companies, poured into Israel; while foreign investments in 1990 were $100 million, they grew twenty times over the following eight years.[36] The transition to a high-tech industry was also enabled by the vast immigration from the former Soviet republics between 1990 and 2000, as two-thirds of the immigrants arriving in Israel were trained in "scientific, technical, or professional sectors".[37]

The Israeli ICT cluster is not, however, unidirectional. For example, among others, Hewlett-Packard and its subsidiaries that develop and produce hardware components in addition to software "are major providers of technological solutions to Israel's system of surveillance and identification".[38]

And perhaps "technological solutions to Israel's system of surveillance" is one of the cues in the Israeli high-tech cluster, as 416 Israeli companies, comprising 21 percent of the high-tech sector, specialize in homeland security – mostly surveillance.[39] For example, so advanced is the Urim SIGINT (signal intelligence) facility of the Israeli army at the Glilot Junction north of Tel Aviv that:

> super-computers garner words and phone numbers "of interest" from intercepted phone calls, e-mails and the mass media as they travel via communication satellites, undersea cables, radio transmissions, or other sources; … where information is collected, translated and passed on to other agencies, including the army and Mossad. … Israel also runs programs of datamining cyberspace.[40]

The development of the ICT cluster in Israel is unique and "[t]he peculiarity of Israel is that the military serves as the foundation of these professional high-tech networks".[41] For example, the Israeli military plays a key role in leading Israeli youth into the field of technology through their elite units 8200 (the unit for electronic warfare), MMRM (the military computer corps), the Signal Corps and other units applying electronics to various degrees.[42] These are the fields where the Israeli graduates with the best grades are being recruited.

The influence of the military should not be underestimated. In addition to training young Israelis in the use of high-technology, "Military research in Israel is acknowledged to be at the forefront in certain areas of communications (especially wireless communications), networks, and data security (especially cryptography)".[43] Furthermore, as the Israeli military does not apply the same copyright laws and protection of intellectual property as a firm would, there is a direct spillover of former officers and Israeli soldiers' knowledge to the high-tech sector when they have finished their service.

This is confirmed by Ori Swed and John Sibley Butler, who state that: "The military was identified both as a significant source of knowledge transfer, and as an eager partner, or as part of governmental investment policy."[44] As for the proportion of military veterans in the Israeli high-tech sector, the veterans comprised 60 percent of the general population, yet they constituted a staggering 90 percent of the high-tech sector. Population groups that have not served in the military are "practically not represented in the industry".[45]

One example of the Israeli military's intellectual spillover to the Israeli ICT cluster is the Israeli company Check Point and their development of VPN-1 – the first commercially available firewall – an idea Gil Shwed, CEO and founder of Check Point, got during his time in the electronic warfare unit 8200.[46] In the early 1990s, as the Internet spread throughout the world within a relatively short time, there were several security concerns and vulnerabilities. However, as Carmel and de Fontenay emphasize: "Almost no tool existed to address these problems before the mid-1990s. And yet the Israeli military had already addressed a number of these problems in its communication networks – and developed tools in response."[47]

Furthermore, Jeff Halper states:

> The ability to surveil under adverse circumstances has long challenged securitization tasks, so the ability of Israeli firms to "borrow" electro-optical, laser and infrared applications from military reconnaissance and avionics applications, together with such military-based technologies as data-mining and intelligence gathering, confer distinct advantages.[48]

The spillover is, as mentioned, not unidirectional, but where the Israeli high-tech industry and army form a symbiotic relationship, it does create tensions:

> Shapira [Israeli State Comptroller] noted the technology crafted by Israeli defense contractors with knowledge developed in the intelligence division. He didn't quantify the damages to the state based on its failure to protect military intellectual property, but the numbers are large enough.[49]

Zeev Pearl, an expert on intellectual property, explained the development where security considerations and non-disclosure were trumped by the commercialization of that know-how.[50]

Thus, to sum up, Israel has moved from the military-industrial to the military–digital complex through:

1. Israeli policies encouraging foreign capital to invest in the Israeli ICT cluster, to a large degree enabled by the peace process in the 1990s.

2. Large-scale immigration of specific human capital from the former Soviet republics.

3. The Israeli military spends vast resources on high-tech, which spills over to the "Silicon Wadi".

This is immensely important to note that, as the Palestinians in the past have fought a superior army in terms of arms and technology, it seems they are now, through hacktivism, once again taking the struggle to another sphere where the Israelis are by far the stronger.

ESCAPING OCCUPATION THROUGH VIRTUALITY

As Israel acquired its first ISP in 1992, and as most Israelis today are online and with an advanced cyber-infrastructure, the growth was initially above average in international comparison, and in 1999 13 percent of the Israeli population used the Internet.[51] Compared to its neighbors in the Middle East, where Internet penetration was still at 1 percent, the development can be considered "skyrocketing". That same year, 1999, the first Palestinian website was created: the website of Birzeit University.

However, as the Internet grew only slowly in the rest of the Arab world because of censorship and dictatorships, poverty and shortage of Arabic language content, the development of a cyber-infrastructure remained slow in the Palestinian areas mainly because

Bezeq – the largest telecommunication company in Israel – had little or no interest in the Palestinians as a market. This was partly due to the Israeli occupation. Before the Oslo Accords, it was illegal for Palestinians to use electronic transmissions due to fears that they might be used as tools in the resistance. This included telephone lines, which are crucial for the development of and access to the Internet.[52]

After the Oslo Accords several Palestinian telecommunication companies were established, with Jawwal having a de facto monopoly. There was – and still is – a dependence on Israeli infrastructure, in most cases owned by Bezeq, where "Calls from one person in the PA [Palestinian Authority] to another in different area code are routed through Israel, as are all international calls".[53] Not only does this have implications for the autonomy of a hypothetical Palestinian state, but also the means are at the disposal of the Israelis to monitor any Palestinian activity in the digital sphere – if measures are not taken by individual Palestinians.

For example, to this day the Israelis are denying Palestinians 3G through Palestinian providers for "security reasons".[54] However, in the summer of 2015 reports surfaced that Palestinian and Israeli authorities were going to sign an agreement allowing for 3G, and perhaps even 4G, technology in the Palestinian territories. It is not clear why the Israelis have suddenly changed their stance, and, as a student at Birzeit University told me: "Imagine if Palestinians could be in a demonstration in Nabi Saleh or any other place and provide the rest of the world a live feed through Twitter or Facebook with information of what is happening. The Israelis would not be happy."[55] Some have explained the Israelis' change of heart as an effort to promote "economic peace" with the Palestinians.[56] Another explanation could also be the fact that social media has shown itself to be incredibly valuable for the Israelis in terms of gathering information. For example, between October 2015 and February 2016 more than 150 arrests took place "based on Facebook posts expressing opinions on the [Palestinian] uprising".[57]

Nevertheless, while 97 out of 100 Palestinians were without a phone and an even larger proportion without Internet in 1996,[58] the numbers rose to 7.5 percent of Palestine's population using the Internet in 2006[59] and jumped to 57.7 percent in 2012.[60]

As has been argued previously, the Internet in the Arab world has been used as a tool for circumventing censorship, avoiding reprisals from repressive regimes, transgressing gender boundaries, getting in touch with the outside world and potentially being used as a weapon (through hacktivism or Internet activism). However, the situation is different in the Palestinian territories where gender boundaries and autocratic rule are not the main issues. Rather, the Internet plays a role in transgressing the physical obstacles of checkpoints, walls, blockades and borders.

Particularly in the case of Palestinian refugees in the diaspora, excluded from their homeland – often only a memory narrated by the older generation – the tension between borders, belonging and attachment is apparent. Thus, cyberspace offers the possibility of transgressing borders and enabling contact with one's own people, in search of news, pictures, videos and other media in determining a person's own identity and sense of belonging.

Yet it should be mentioned – after the construction of the wall which began in 2002, the blockade of Gaza since 2007, and encirclement of cities such as Qalqiliya (in addition to the countless curfews) – that virtuality is also a means of transgressing the limitations on movement within Palestine. Although, I should note, they are not in the same situation of displacement as their Palestinian families in the diaspora. We can, in other words, talk about virtuality in a situation of increased isolation – not just from the outside world but also from the rest of the Palestinian community.

Also, as I concentrate on hacktivism and cyber-resistance, the Internet as it emerged in Palestine was not just a tool to keep in touch with friends and relatives by transgressing physical borders but also a tool to influence the narrative – that is, the Internet extended to being a means for the struggle for hegemony.

The Italian Marxist Antonio Gramsci's theory of hegemony tried to explain how the ruling capitalist class so successfully kept control over the working class for centuries. The main premise is that brute force alone cannot be enough to retain power, but it also requires the control of ideas.[61] The same can be applied to the occupation of Palestine where there is, to a large degree, an ongoing war of hegemony between the Palestinians and Israelis about the foundation of the conflict and the right of existence.

This was apparent in the summer of 2014 during the latest bombardment of Gaza, operation Protective Edge, where the two Twitter hash-tags "#IsraelUnderFire" (pro-Israeli) and "#SaveGaza" (pro-Palestinian) were the most frequent to influence the narrative of the ongoing horrors. Thus, there are several means of moving

Palestinian political activity to the virtual realm besides hacktivism: Internet activism and attempts at changing the narrative discourse are examples.

It is possible to see Palestinian hacktivism involving the defacement of Israeli websites in this context, where the main goal is not only to raise awareness, but also to present the Palestinian narrative to an audience that otherwise would not be exposed to it – especially under an occupation where counter-narratives exist, but are nevertheless mute:

> Also, the reality that Israeli commentators appear more on [American] television than Palestinian ones showed a pattern of support for Israel. More surveys and content analyses showed that even when presenting the Palestinian point of view, it was prominent Israelis who often did the writing, underlining the extent to which Palestinians are not permitted to speak on their own behalf but must be represented by others, if at all.[62]

Thus, Palestinian hacktivism can be seen as something more than a tool to cause physical and economic damage to what the hackers deem the occupation's infrastructure. Palestinian hacktivism is also about creating a narrative through counter-publics where none exists.[63] Palestinian hacktivism gives a voice to the voiceless by creating autonomous subjects by occupying and recreating foreign spaces.

4

THE ISTISHHĀDĪ AND THE EMERGENCE OF PALESTINIAN ELECTRONIC JIHAD

When the negotiations with Israel failed in the late 1990s, the Palestinian people and movement were left disillusioned and with little faith in the international community's ability to help end the conflict. Combined with the daily frustrations and the sense that they were being tricked by Israel and the international society – with the continuous growth of settlements and the Israelis' apparent unwillingness to withdraw from the Palestinian territories – demonstrations and popular grassroots resistance emerged in the same way as before the First Intifada. In fact, the Second Intifada was so closely connected to the failure of Oslo that by some it was called the Oslo War.

Yet these demonstrations drew a harsh response from the Israelis, where small arms fire was answered with tanks and artillery shelling of civilian Palestinian areas.[1] It was so brutal that to call it Israeli state violence would be an understatement. During just the three first weeks of the Second Intifada one million rounds of ammunition were fired against the Palestinians,[2] and, at the end of the intifada, the results were:

> more than 3,300 Palestinians killed, at least 85 percent of them civilians. Some 650 were children and youths, half under the age of 15. In 88 percent of the incidents in which children were killed, there was no direct confrontation with Israeli soldiers. Another 50,000 Palestinians were injured, 20 percent of whom were children and youths. Some 2,500 civilians were permanently disabled.[3]

Thus, while the First Intifada was popular and to a large extent non-violent, the second became militarized, where the Palestinians also armed themselves to conduct, for example, suicide bombings and shooting operations against Israeli soldiers, settlers and civilians.

What is important to note is that with the death of the Oslo Accords and the militarization of the Second Intifada, another evident change in the narrative of the resistance's agent emerged: from the passive shahīd of the First Intifada to that of the active subject of al-istishhādī ("the martyrdom-seeker").[4] Initially, the Islamist movements had conducted suicide bombings while the rest of the Palestinian political spectrum was committed to negotiations throughout the 1990s. However, with the rise of the Second Intifada most of the political groupings chose to adopt the strategy whether Islamist (Hamas and Palestinian Islamic Jihad), secular (Fatah) or Marxist-Leninist (PFLP). The use of the suicide bomber who *actively* sought martyrdom can be seen as a return to the roots of the resistance, when only direct pressure and violence were regarded as sufficient to put pressure on the Zionist project.[5]

This explanation of the istishhādī's emergence cannot be the only explanation, of course, but has also been described by Nasser Abufarha in his elaborate study of Palestinian suicide bombers as mimetic violence, an attempt to "mime" the same violence and breach of normality that the Palestinians felt they faced under the Israeli occupation.[6] Through the bombing of restaurants, coffee shops and buses the Israelis would be abruptly pulled out of their sense of normality and security. If the Palestinians could not feel any kind of security or know when the next Israeli shelling was going to hit their neighborhood, they would make sure that the Israelis would feel the same sense of insecurity.

Yet, although the mere eruption of the intifada came as a result of the Oslo Accords, not ending but rather cementing the occupation, and the disproportionately violent reprisals of the Israelis contributed to its militarization (and thus to the istishhādī discourse), it is worth considering the inability of the Palestinian political class to prevent it. For example, there had been significant changes in the Palestinian political fabric where, Darweish and Rigby emphasize, "the cadres from the [first] intifada followed different trajectories, but two career paths were common. Some joined the new PA, whilst others founded or joined non-governmental organisations concerned with themes like democratisation and peace-building".[7] The potential Palestinian leadership, that could have led an unarmed popular resistance, was thus lost. Admittedly, the rivalry between Fatah and Hamas fed this development.

There can be little doubt that this militarization of the intifada was a godsend for the Israelis in terms of framing the occupation. With the terror attacks on the World Trade Center in 2001, the Cold War was replaced by a "Huntingtonian" narrative of the clash of civilizations – first and foremost between the "civilized" West and Muslims through the so-called "War on Terror". It was the consolidation of the neo-orientalist narrative of Israel as a Western outpost struggling against the brutal hordes of Muslims who did not want to see anything but the blood of Israelis.

As Robert D. Kaplan himself described Israel, it was a "fortress amid a vast and volatile realm of Islam".[8] So within days after 11 September 2001, the military attacks on Palestinians intensified, with the subsequent construction of a new discourse where, according to Ariel Sharon, the resistance of Palestinians was not that different from the means of terror used by Usama Bin Laden.[9] Furthermore, Sharon stated that this was not just about defending Israeli civilians but a situation where "The fight against terror is an international struggle of the free world against the forces of darkness who seek to destroy our liberty and our way of life".[10]

Although the end date of the intifada is disputed, whether with Yasir Arafat's death or the Israeli "disengagement" from Gaza, nevertheless, after six years the use of suicide bombers ended – with one exceptional case in 2007. The end of the Second Intifada must partly be seen in the context of the suffering the Palestinians had to endure. For example, the older generations in the West Bank and Gaza have shown themselves to be rather reluctant regarding a third intifada, as they fear it will be closer to the Second Intifada and its violence, than to the first.

Another factor in the end of the intifada was the National Conciliation Document for Prisoners – also named the Palestinian Prisoner's Document – signed by the major political parties (Fatah, Hamas, PFLP, DFLP and Palestinian Islamic Jihad). The document represented a change in the Palestinian resistance's struggle against the Israeli occupation: While some have explained the end of Palestinian suicide bombings as a mark of the success of the separation wall, Shin Bet has emphasized the importance of the Palestinian truce, and Hamas and other factions' active decision to focus on the political scene.[11] So far, the relative calm has persisted to this day, while the exceptions have been the bombardments of Gaza and the intensification of protests in the West Bank.

THE ELECTRONIC JIHADISTS ARE COMING

So during this continuous development and change of the highly multifaceted Palestinian resistance, how and when did Palestinian hacktivism emerge?

As we have seen, the development of the Palestinian resistance moved from pinprick operations from neighboring Arab countries to the resistance re-emerging in the Palestinian territories after the defeat of the PLO – with the transformation of the fidā'ī into the shahīd. With the failure of the Oslo process, and the collapse of faith in the international community, the passive shahīd transformed itself into the active subject of al-istishhādī. However, with their second failure to liberate themselves during the Second Intifada, this strategy was also left behind. It is within this framework that electronic jihad and cyberwar emerged between Israel and the Palestinians:

Though it is hard to point to the exact dates for different events and the establishment of different hacktivist groups and cyber-departments in armed brigades such as Hamas and Islamic Jihad, most likely the phenomenon emerged and developed in the late 1990s. As mentioned in the introduction, one of the earliest known encounters Israel had in what has been called the "nearest thing to all-out cyberwar" was on 6 October 2000.

We should note how the "cyberwar" coincided with the Second Intifada as hacktivists sympathetic to the Palestinians on that date defaced 40 Israeli websites in a couple of hours.[12] Israeli hackers responded and started DDoSing Palestinian and Arab websites. As the story goes, one of these websites was none other than that of Hizbollah. The Israeli hack of Hizbollah's website led to what has been described as a wave of calls for "cyber-jihad" against Israel, and a new round of counterattacks against Israel brought down, among others, the websites of the Knesset, the Ministry of Foreign Affairs, the Bank of Israel and the Tel Aviv Stock Exchange.[13]

It could best be described as a game of cat and mouse, where Hizbollah established new mirrors of its website,[14] which were subsequently replaced by Israel with pictures of the Star of David and Hebrew text. In the meantime, Palestinian hackers took down still more Israeli government websites.[15]

What is striking with this sudden escalation is that already, from the beginning, the hacking and counter-hacking of Israeli and

Arab websites was not limited to Palestinians and Israelis, but rather expressed itself as an Arab–Israeli cyberwar, leading to a surge of cyber-counterattacks from all over the Muslim world.

For example, an Arab group calling itself UNITY took a leading role in the cyberwar, in addition to the Islamic Gateway World Wide Media Network, which participated in several DDoS attacks. This spilled over to the American cyber-domain, where the website of the Israeli lobby group AIPAC was hacked by a Pakistani hacker who called himself Dr Nuker;[16] he defaced the website and published the credit card numbers and email addresses of several APAIC members.[17] Even the Israeli military unit for maintaining computer security, Aftahat Ma'Khvehim, reported that most of the attacks came from Lebanon and the Gulf States.[18]

From July 1999 to mid-April 2002, 548 Israeli domain websites were hacked and defaced.[19] The CEO of the Israeli ISP Netvision, Gilad Rabinovich, said himself that the so-called "inter-fada" (combining the two words *Internet* and *intifada*) was started by the Israelis: "How did the story start? We [the Israelis] started it. It was so sexy – let's put an Israeli flag on the Hizbollah site. And then they woke up."[20]

These figures show implicitly that though the average Internet penetration in Israel and Palestine had not reached its full potential, they were nevertheless already able to use the cybersphere as an area for digital warfare in 1999.

As it would be a seemingly impossible task to list every single attack and counterattack in the Palestinian/Israeli cybersphere – in addition to the fact that most likely a majority of them go unnoticed

– it is worth pointing out that the number of attacks and escalations have coincided and risen according to the situation on the ground: when there has been intensified conflict between the Palestinians and Israelis on the ground, with events such as the attacks on Gaza, the Second Intifada and the 2006 Lebanon War, cyberattacks on Israel have subsequently peaked. One example is late December 2008 when the Israel Defense Forces (IDF) hacked the television station of Hamas, broadcasting an animated series portraying the deaths of the Hamas leadership with the caption "Time is running out".[21]

The escalation in the cybersphere according to the situation on the ground is not limited to escalations in the Palestinian/Israeli context, but also in the Muslim world at large. For example, when various publications have mocked the Muslims' Prophet Muhammad, this has also led to a series of corresponding cyberattacks. One example is the al-Qassam Cyber Fighters launching Operation Ababil as a protest against the video *Innocence of Muslims* in 2012, disrupting the websites of the New York Stock Exchange and a number of banks such as J. P. Morgan Chase and the Bank of America. Although acknowledging that it was easy to dismiss the manifesto of the group, Rodney Joffe, senior vice president at Sterling, stated that "I think we learned our lessons with the al-Qassam Cyber Fighters … and it's been brutally damaging".[22] It was in this timeframe that we saw the emergence of several Palestinian hacktivist teams, such as Gaza Hacker Team (2007), Gaza Security Team (2008) and KDMS Team (2013).

There are no clear answers as to why so many Palestinian hacktivist teams emerged in this period. Most likely it can be attributed to high levels of education and high unemployment rates combined with technological developments enabling the Palestinians to follow the trajectory of electronic jihad. For example, in 2007 the unemployment rate (fifteen years and above) was 21.5 percent for all of the Palestinian territories.[23] Additionally, in Gaza (which, as we will see, is the most vibrant of the Palestinian areas for hacktivism) the unemployment rate was 29.7 percent.[24] Furthermore, only 29.5 percent of the entire Palestinian population could be considered as being in full employment (working 35 hours and above per week).[25]

These unemployment rates were combined with a high level of education, with an adult literacy rate (population fifteen years and above) of 94.4 percent in 2007,[26] and an enrollment rate for secondary education of 91 percent in 2008/2009 – a figure which puts Palestine in the lead in the Middle East and North Africa region.[27] Furthermore, the enrollment of young people aged between eighteen and twenty-four in tertiary education was 33 percent in the same period – higher than the average for middle-income countries.[28]

Thus, the impact of the Internet – and with it the change in the possibilities for political action – combined with a highly educated Palestinian population that to a large degree is unemployed and under occupation, might be the decisive factors for the emergence of hacktivism in Palestine.

Furthermore, when it comes to the electronic warfare units of Hamas and Islamic Jihad, the way Islamist movements have considered engineering and technical professions important should be emphasized. For example, Diego Gambetta and Steffen Hertog state that "[e]ngineers are indeed overrepresented among violent Islamic radicals by two to four times the size we would expect"[29] and "[a]mong the 42 of the 78 cases for whom we could find out the precise discipline, three types of engineering predominate: electrical and civil engineering, and computer-related studies".[30]

Yet it is easy to forget, as we focus solely on different hacktivist groups clashing with each other, that the cyberwar led by and conducted against Israel also lies on a nation-state level. We should not forget one of the most lethal malwares – in the least literal sense of the term – ever deployed: the Stuxnet computer worm which struck the Iranian nuclear facility. The worm was so sophisticated and unprecedented that it was described as nothing but a "military-grade cyber missile".[31] In short, the worm was designed to hit the uranium-enriching centrifuges of the Iranian nuclear plants. Yet it was picky about its targets. In order to create the worst possible damage with the utmost effectiveness, it was necessary to limit its spread: only those controllers produced by Siemens were hit.[32]

Suddenly, the spinning centrifuges at Natanz uranium enrichment facility, to mention but one of them, would be subjected to increased pressure while at the same time the control room would show that everything was running smoothly by replaying the previous recordings of the plant's system values.[33] In the end it destroyed 1,000 out of Iran's 6,000 uranium-enriching centrifuges and thus was possibly the first cyberattack with the sole purpose of actual physical damage.

Although no one has claimed responsibility for the worm, it is a badly hidden secret that it was most likely the result of American–Israeli cooperation. According to the US whistleblower and former CIA employee Edward Snowden, it was none other than the National Security Agency (NSA), under the Foreign Affairs Directorate, and Israel that had designed, co-written and executed the attack.[34] Furthermore, the worm required that someone injected it using USB sticks and local networks. Again, the CIA and the Israelis were allegedly responsible for gaining entry to the plant so it could be done – with the help of "unwitting accomplices – engineers, plant technicians".[35]

That there is an actually ongoing cyberwar is hardly a surprise but, as pointed out by Farwell and Rohozinski, what makes Stuxnet interesting is how it redefines what we see as the use of force or an armed attack between nations.[36] For example; the Stuxnet did not injure, disable or kill anyone, although it intended to cause physical damage, and succeeded in doing so. Is then cyberwar only equivalent to an armed attack when it kills someone? Few would dispute that would in fact be the case if we saw the hacking of an airplane's control systems which deliberately led it to crash into a building or the taking down of the power grid necessary to keep a hospital running and thus endangering the lives of patients. But what about simply taking down websites, factories or, as with Stuxnet, nuclear facilities?

We will return to that later, yet it is worth emphasizing how these "tools" are becoming increasingly sophisticated, as was the case with the Stuxnet-related malware Duqu, which targeted the Iranian Oil Ministry and the national oil company in 2012. Furthermore, with the involvement of the CIA, NSA and the Israeli military, Flame, the state-sponsored espionage malware, was hailed as the, at the time, "most sophisticated cyber-weapon yet unleashed":

Flame was capable of stealing data from infected computers, logging keystrokes, activating computer microphones to record conversations, and taking screen shots. What made it so effective was its ability to constantly evolve in order to send home intelligence to an unknown spy-master controlling servers around the world. Then, once it needed to be extracted, the virus could clean out the inside of a computer where it had been hiding, leaving behind no evidence that it had ever been activated.[37]

PART II

PALESTINE 2.0 AND THE NEW CYBER-WARRIORS

5

GAZA HACKER TEAM: ELECTRONIC JIHADISTS AND SCRIPT KIDDIES

"Yahya! Yahya! Come quickly! They have replied! They actually replied!" I was running through our flat outside of Ramallah as one of the biggest breakthroughs had been realized. "Wallah? Let me see…" He read through the email before he looked at me. "Is that it…?" "Well, yeah, but… They replied!"

Of course, Yahya, my roommate, was not too impressed, and rightly so. The answers I had got from Gaza Hacker Team, more specifically mr.leon, were pretty much limited to being either "yes", "no" or "We are Palestinians". They had filled in their short answers under each question. But, I reminded myself, it was nevertheless a breakthrough.

However, it was not without problems. The following day, I lost access to my email account. Everything else worked perfectly fine, student email, Facebook, the whole shebang, but my personal email? Nothing. It was probably just a blunder by the host server, I figured, as happens on a regular basis when Facebook goes down for a couple of hours and you suddenly have no idea what to do with your life.

Yet when I was able to access my email, however unstable, I received notifications of unusual login patterns and had to answer several security questions. As I tried to find out what the problem could be, I checked my Gmail activity and found out that there were several logins from both the Gaza Strip starting the day after I sent the email to mr.leon and from Tel Aviv four days after the email was sent.

Was it Gaza Hacker Team? I have no idea, although I do understand they might have wanted to check if I actually was the master's student I presented myself as. Was it the Israelis who had hacked my account? Most likely, but then again, they are sufficiently tech-savvy for it not to show in my login pattern, and then certainly not from Tel Aviv of all places. After some consideration, I carefully and politely asked mr.leon if it was they who had hacked my email account. "We do not do that kind of stuff", he replied. Perhaps not too convincing coming from someone with the word "Hacker" in their team name.

FORMATION AND BELONGING

23 October 2012: the Israeli police finds out all of its computers have been infiltrated and compromised. Worst of all, it has taken them a whole week to find out and the malware has spread to other Israeli government departments. The result is taking down all the servers of the Israeli police, cutting off Internet access and banning the use of USB sticks – which lasts for an additional week.[1] In February 2014, two years later, the same thing happens again as hackers breach the Civil Administration of Judea and Samaria, the government agency

that deals with all administrative matters in area A in the West Bank.[2] Later, according to the network security company FireEye, the attacks are linked to Gaza Hacker Team.[3]

Little has been written about this peculiar team, which has existed for almost a decade now. According to themselves, the team was established in 2007,[4] but it is difficult to find attacks from that year and the frequency and strength of the attacks seems to have been rather low for the first few years. One of the earliest reports of their successful attacks was that of the Israeli Kadima party – then led by the Israeli Prime Minister Ehud Olmert – on 13 February 2008. Yet by 2012 Gaza Hacker Team had developed and managed to make several headlines in Israel and the rest of the world with thousands of sites hacked.

During the interviews with Gaza Hacker Team, mr.leon explained the composition and organization of the group, which can be described as the following with a top-down hierarchy:

1. The leadership (al-qiyāda) consisting of three persons: mr.leon, Casper and Claw. All of them are Palestinians and residing in the Gaza Strip.
2. The team (al-farīq), which constitutes the whole Gaza Hacker Team, and for which the leadership is responsible. The members of the team are Palestinians in addition to several "associates" – hackers from other Arab countries.
3. Groups (majmūʿāt) which are specialized in their respective field, as one group's responsibility is to attack the website itself (majmūʿā ikhtirāq al-mawāqiʿ), while

another group has the responsibility of hacking the setup and emails (majmū'ā ikhtirāq al-ajhiza wa al-īmaylāt).

Thus, they explained that all the necessary experience was combined in the team.

However, mr.leon did emphasize that even though they were in the same team, not all the members knew each other and were only in touch through the use of the forum and various communication tools on the Internet. Thus, the organization of the hacktivists has a clear resemblance to other resistance groups and brigades in the line of organizational structure and secrecy – in order not to potentially compromise the rest of the organization.

An example is Palestinian Islamic Jihad, which operates with several cells within a hierarchy: one person in a particular cell (the middle man/mediator) knows one person in another cell above, but not the rest of its members. In that cell, again, another mediator has contact with another cell, but not the rest of its members. Hence, if one cell gets compromised the whole structure of the organization will not be threatened. The same theoretically applies to Gaza Hacker Team.

It should, however, be emphasized that this kind of organizational structure is not limited to Palestinian brigades. All of these features (cell divisions, anonymity and limited contact across organizational units or divisions) are rather typical of clandestine organizations which in the majority of the cases are motivated by the need for security. The dilemma is usually that more open organizational structures allow a better flow of information and a greater efficiency, but simultaneously become more vulnerable to repression. As we have seen, efficiency and safety are two priorities that have to be weighed against each other.

Yet we should not take the similarities too far, as if Gaza Hacker Team suddenly emerges as some bizarre online version of Palestinian Islamic Jihad. The resemblance is there, but it is simultaneously a feature of organizing anonymously on the Internet where the anonymous nature of the Internet itself makes it possible.

As with other hacktivist groups such as KDMS Team, to which I will return later, Gaza Hacker Team made it perfectly clear that it did not have any membership of or affiliation with Palestinian political parties: "We do not belong to any movement … We are youth from Gaza."[5] This included emphasizing that they did not have any support from any political faction, group or movement nor did they have any interest in cooperating with any group other than hacktivist teams from within Palestine and outside, including the Arab world and the rest of the global cyber-community.

A personal friend of mine, and fatḥāwī (Fatah-member) since childhood, described the statements as "tactically smart and very clever": Gaza Hacker Team was not affiliating itself with a political movement that could brand it and subsequently alienate other Palestinians with a different political view.[6] He considered it a move to gain political support from the entire Palestinian community.

It should nevertheless be noted that at the end of 2014/ beginning of 2015 the first thing that welcomed you on the Gaza Hacker Team's forum[7] was two soldiers with the headbands of the Izz al-Din al-Qassam Brigade and the al-Quds Brigade – the armed factions of Hamas and Islamic Jihad. However, as I discuss later on, this does not mean that Gaza Hacker Team has a secret affiliation with these two parties. Rather it represents a certain approach and way to brand itself in the struggle against the occupation. Furthermore, it should be noted that the header of the website is constantly being changed.

Nevertheless, Palestinian hacktivism as an independent factor is a feature within the Palestinian resistance which could possibly transcend the notion of political parties (including their armed brigades) alone being the main agents for the liberation of the homeland – where resistance is not only a duty but also a possibility for every Palestinian who wishes to be involved. Thus, the hackers in Gaza Hacker Team seemingly recreate and transform themselves from "normal and unimportant" Palestinian youths to autonomous subjects in the resistance where the universal right to resist occupation is not limited to and/or monopolized by decisions made in political parties such as Hamas, Fatah, PFLP, PLO and others. When one loses the belief in the political parties' ability to be agents of resistance, this should create a breeding ground for independent, spontaneous movements that are not at the mercy of the Palestinian political establishment.

It should be emphasized that this development is nothing new in Palestine, nor is it limited to Palestinian hacktivists. One example is from 2011, as a new and different youth current emerged in Gaza with the name Gaza Youth Breaks Out (GYBO). Drawing the attention of the whole world, the group refused to have any links with the Palestinian establishment and criticized it heavily. In their manifesto the group condemned the Israeli occupation, but also the corruption and incompetence of Fatah and Hamas, stating: "Fuck Israel. Fuck Hamas. Fuck Fatah."[8]

The frustration is not limited to Gaza, of course, where the lack of trust in the Palestinian Authority and the leadership has led many to predict that a third intifada will not be directed towards the Israeli occupation alone, but first and foremost against the Palestinian leadership which sold out. As one of countless taxi drivers expressed it on the road between Ramallah and Jerusalem, "First we end the sulṭa, the PA, and then the occupation".[9]

It might seem like a watershed in the belief system of the Palestinians, yet we tend to forget the experiences of the past, specifically the already mentioned First Intifada, as it also simultaneously functioned as a "house-cleaning operation" as the Palestinians resisted the occupation; first and foremost, the "house-cleansing" was a removal of Palestinian collaborators who cooperated with the Israeli Civil Administration, and strong pressure was applied to them. Several of the Palestinian leaders in Palestine at the time were also loyal to the Jordanian King Hussein instead of the Palestinian cause. Norman Finkelstein writes about his 1988 meeting with mayor al-Khalīl of Hebron, noting the mayor stated that "98 percent of the Palestinians" want King Hussein as their leader.[10]

It should be emphasized that the Palestinian youth's lack of faith in the traditional political parties in Palestine and their way of organizing is a result of a longstanding development in the Palestinian political scene – which could partly explain why the Palestinian hacktivists lack interest in engaging with them. As it is highly likely that the hackers are young adults, since they refer to themselves as shabāb, this factor must be seen in the context of the young average age of the Palestinian population.

As the average age in the Palestinian territories in 2014 was 20.7,[11] the average age of the Palestinian political leadership is disproportionally high. The best example is the Palestinian president, Mahmoud Abbas, who is fifty-nine years older than the average age. This has to a large degree alienated the Palestinian youth, and the next generation that is likely to take over the leadership is approximately in their sixties (one of the candidates suggested as being Abbas' successor, however unlikely, is sixty-two-year-old Salam Fayyad).

This is in addition to the persisting nepotism and corruption in the Palestinian political sphere, where both Fatah and Hamas have created authoritarian regimes in the West Bank and Gaza. It is that factor that has alienated the Palestinian youth, and not the split between the parties itself. While the Palestinians during the First Intifada had only one external threat, they now face three: the occupation, Hamas and Fatah, where the latter two do not accept any challenges to their rule and dealings with Israel.[12]

The anger, frustration and at times apathy towards the authoritarian rule of Hamas and Fatah, often justified by the necessity of "responsible ruling" with the PA–Israeli security cooperation preventing a third intifada on the PA-led road to liberation is, although it was written in a different time, captured in Bertolt Brecht's poem "The Interrogation of the Good":

Step forward: we hear

That you are a good man.

You cannot be bought, but the lightning

Which strikes the house, also

Cannot be bought.

You hold to what you said.

But what did you say?

You are honest, you say your opinion.

Which opinion?

You are brave.

Against whom?

You are wise.

For whom?

You do not consider your personal advantages.

Whose advantages do you consider then?

You are a good friend.

Are you also a good friend of the good people?

Hear us then: we know

You are our enemy. This is why we shall

Now put you in front of a wall. But in consideration of your

   merits and good qualities

We shall put you in front of a good wall and shoot you

With a good bullet from a good gun and bury you

With a good shovel in the good earth.[13]

Yet perhaps, and only in addition, this is not just a feature of the alien-ated Palestinian youth of which Gaza Hacker Team is also a part, but also the nature of the current hacktivist ethos. The different hacktivist teams of the world, and I am here excluding state-sponsored hackers, are not famous for reaching out and organizing meetings with the political elite in order to agree coordination, compromise and what we might call "responsible" tactics and political channels. Hacktivism, after all, is still a bit too unruly, and it would seem ludicrous to believe that a hacker group such as Anonymous, in a dimension where it had a formally established leadership, would start cooperating with some-one such as the American politician Bernie Sanders.

To illustrate the lack of a will to cooperate, when I inter-viewed the Syrian Electronic Army – a Syrian state-sponsored hacktivist team loyal to the Bashar al-Assad regime – they stated that Palestine was "the heart of the Arab nation" and thus it was manda-tory to defend it from the Israeli occupiers. Yet they had no plans to cooperate with the Palestinian teams when they attacked the Israeli cyber-infrastructure.[14]

THE GOALS OF GAZA HACKER TEAM AND A POSSIBLE NUCLEAR LEAK AT DIMONA

The secretive organizational structure of Gaza Hacker Team does remind one of the structures of other armed groups with their cell hierarchy and limited, open contact with one another. However, what might be more interesting is the way the members of Gaza Hacker Team perceive themselves: mainly as a part of the armed Palestinian struggle.[15] This does explain the way they appear to the outside world with images of armed and masked men on their website – instead of misunderstanding their cultural expression as some form of political affiliation. One example is the avatars used by many of the forum participants, where two out of the three leaders, mr.leon[16] and Casper,[17] had, at the time of writing in 2014, avatars of soldiers holding rifles, thus reshaping and promoting themselves as soldiers in the struggle against the occupation.

Yet the most interesting place to find some essential information about Gaza Hacker Team is in its program of principles. It not only tells us something about the self-perception of the group, but also its goals and ideology:

The preface to the document, which defines modern, electronic warfare and the necessity for Muslims to take part in it, states the importance of the Internet and the potential damage caused by disrupting its use.[18] Furthermore, Chapter 1 ("The definition of Gaza Hacker Team") explicitly states that the goal of hacking enemy websites is to inflict economic damage: "The yearly loss of millions of dollars as a result of the operations where websites are hacked and destroyed."[19]

The argument of Gaza Hacker Team is that the hosts of the websites or the owners of the servers are forced to hire programmers to secure the website and remove the potential loopholes, which increases their expenses. The goal of harming the targets economically was also confirmed during the interviews with Gaza Hacker Team, as the leadership stated that this was one of several objectives of the cyberwarfare.[20]

Inflicting economic damage could be done by obstructing daily life and causing problems for the hosts of the websites because of the uncertainty of access for the users. Thus, it is not necessary for Gaza Hacker Team to inflict direct economic damage on the websites themselves, but to create such uncertainty among the users of the particular website that tension and lack of efficiency will be created.

It is, in general, among the most severe damage that hacktivism and cyberwarfare can inflict, if done right; this was elaborated upon by Ash Patel from the Finnish company for network security, Stonesoft – acquired in 2013 by the antivirus company MacAfee – when he described DDoS attacks against UK websites:

> The DDoS attacks also have the potential to damage the reputation of "UK PLC" – which is currently promoting itself as the place to do online business. The government should be showing that this is a reliable country for companies to operate in. But such attacks portray the UK negatively and can affect how many businesses trade both in and with the UK.[21]

Consequentially, if the Palestinian hacktivists – with or without support from outside – are able to maintain a stable and high rate of attacks against Israeli websites over a period of time it might affect the reputation of Israeli servers and cyber-domains to such a degree that investments decrease, and thus affect the Israeli economy as a whole.

Evidently, it is hard to establish figures on how much cyberattacks on Israel affect the economy, and Israel is not known to make public attacks that have not led to the loss of human lives. Yet there are examples of how much it *can* cost. In February 2013 an unknown group of hackers managed to close off a tunnel in Haifa for two days in a row as they hacked its security cameras.[22] The first attack did not last for more than twenty minutes, while the second lasted for eight whole hours. The estimated costs of the attack amounted to hundreds of thousands of dollars, which is rather costly for an attack lasting approximately an average working day. Try to add that to all of the attacks conducted annually and you would get a sense of the costs inflicted.

On the other hand, Gaza Hacker Team stated that it was important to convey a message during special events that could highlight what was going on.[23] Therefore, there is an aspect of information warfare where the daily lives of Israelis and their normality is interrupted by being confronted with pictures and other forms of documentation from Gaza, showing what is actually happening, as pictures of dead women and children are popping up instead of the online bank account they expected to see. To use Gaza Hacker Team's own words about the psychological warfare that electronic jihad constitutes: "[i]t kills the morale of the enemy, injures his mind and terrorizes his people and soldiers".[24]

The goals can in other words be summarized as imposing economic damage (directly and indirectly), disrupting Israeli daily life by closing off access to necessary websites such as bank accounts and information, and conducting information warfare by spreading awareness of current events such as during the escalations in Gaza.

If we compare Gaza Hacker Team's perception of itself as the continuation of the Palestinian armed resistance in cyberspace and its goals of conduct, it is interesting to note the goals in the traditional armed resistance. For example, during an interview with a militant in the al-Aqsa Martyrs' Brigade – Fatah's armed wing – he never mentioned specific consequences, but chose to sum up the armed operations as scare tactics – mainly to push the occupation back to the negotiation table: "Our goals, for the al-Aqsa brigades, were scare-goals to any occupied people in the world, and thank God we are the last occupied people in the world. We depict and describe ourselves as fighters for peace."[25]

Thus it is obvious that although the means of the al-Aqsa Brigade and Gaza Hacker Team are different, their effects share the common traits of psychological warfare, though applying it through qualitatively disparate spheres of struggle on the ground and in the virtual realm. Yet, for now, we should not be too quick to define Gaza Hacker Team as a continuation of the armed brigades. It is never that simple, as I will show later.

For Islamic Jihad, on the other hand, the perspective was different. Yes, the tools differed, but the notion of the "electronic war" was intrinsically connected to the physical struggle on the ground. One aspect was the assistance of the hackers in Islamic Jihad working on tracing and monitoring Israeli soldiers, another was direct sabotage through, for example, jamming phone lines to complicate the work of the occupation.[26]

There is, however, still the elephant in the room: the issue of hacking as psychological warfare. Ever had your Facebook account hacked? It is rather distressing. Yet the term "psychological warfare" does unfortunately imply some kind of connection to terrorism as the main goal of the latter is to instill fear into a population or government in order that they will grant the perpetrator's demands. We should, for the sake of the argument, focus on the mimetic violence which can both be included in and excluded from the sphere of terrorism.

One example is the DDoS attacks on the Israeli El Al Airlines and the Tel Aviv Stock Exchange – this time not conducted by Palestinian hacktivists, but by the Saudi-based Oxomar mentioned briefly in the introduction – as the attacks seem to have made an impression regarding Israel as the technological superpower and the biggest producer of firewall and anti-virus technology. The Israeli Minister of Improvement of Government Service Michael Eitan stated that the attack gave no reason to worry, though interestingly enough the Israeli news site Ynetnews started the article with the question "Cybersafe?"[27] Marc Goldberg, blogging for the Israeli newspaper *Jerusalem Post* stated that the attacks "have shown us just how vulnerable we are to individuals operating thousands of miles away".[28] Last, but not least, the Israeli blogger "Carl in Jerusalem", running the blog *Israel Matzav*, finished one of his blog posts with the rhetorical question: "Aren't we supposed to have the best Internet security in the world?"[29]

These could be used as textbook examples of how mimetic violence works: it does not necessarily mean that any Israelis are sitting in their living room fearing for their lives, but that the normalcy of Israeli daily lives has been interrupted as they suddenly realize that there is something going on from which they cannot fully protect themselves. Thus, the attacks cannot merely be defined by the economic damage it inflicts on the Israeli enemy but also by the uncertainty and unpredictability of the hacktivist attacks that constitute its core premise. One can simply never know when a vital part of the Israel cyber-infrastructure will be taken down.

The unpredictability of cyberattacks and the uncertainty is, however, only one aspect of it, whereas the fabrication of false information to confuse and even create panic has also been used as a means. During the latest escalation in Gaza during the summer 2014 with Operation Protective Edge, the Twitter account of the Israel Defense Forces published a message in English that reached the whole world: "#WARNING: Possible nuclear leak in the region after 2 rockets hit Dimona nuclear facility."[30]

A couple of hours later the same account published an apology. It had been hacked and the Israel Defense Forces had regained control of the account, and the situation too for that matter. Furthermore, the IDF would continue the combat against terrorism on all fronts "[i]ncluding the cyber dimension".[31] Yet it should be mentioned that the hack, which was quite clever, albeit bizarre, was not done by Gaza Hacker Team, but the aforementioned Syrian Electronic Army.

On the issue of hacktivism as a continuation of the armed struggle, Palestinian hacktivism is implicitly being confirmed as precisely that by the way the Israeli government and the Israel Defense Forces have responded to the cyber-threat posed by Palestinian and other hacktivists – which means hacktivist attacks are seen as an issue for the Israeli army. One example is how they have defined cyberwarfare as the fifth realm of warfare alongside sea, air, land and space, with special cyber-forces to counter the attacks;[32] the office of Israeli Prime Minister Benyamin Netanyahu stating in September 2014 that:

I decided last week to develop a national authority on the cyber issue to arrange and see to defending the entire State of Israel on the cyber issue. That is, defending not only important facilities and security agencies, but how to defend Israeli citizens against these attacks. … It is, in effect, the creation of an air force against new threats and not rely on this being carried out by existing agencies. We are in a new world; we are preparing with new forces.[33]

To sum up, Gaza Hacker Team's goals can be described as inflicting direct and indirect economic damage on Israeli websites, spreading information about the ongoing events in the Palestinian territories and applying mimetic violence to breach Israelis' sense of normalcy in their daily lives. Furthermore, their electronic hacktivist campaigns are interestingly rendered by both Gaza Hacker Team and the Israeli state as military warfare.

BYPASSING THE IRON DOME: SCRIPT KIDDIES AND PORNOGRAPHY

The chapter was introduced by Gaza Hacker Team's hack of the Israeli police in 2012 and the Civil Administration of Judea and Samaria two years later in 2014. So how was it done?

It is easy to think that if all loopholes are secured and the newest antivirus technology is installed, one will be secure from all external threats. However, as we know, everything and anything can be hacked; even where we are the most exposed: our toilets.[34] The question is not whether something gets hacked, but how and when. After all, cybersecurity is not limited to that of technology. For when all is said and done, everything can be compromised by human interaction and reason (or rather, the lack of reason). For instance, what all of the infiltrations of the Israeli police and civil administrations had in common was the fact that the malware was enabled by an employee opening a malicious document sent – in most cases – by email. Simply put, what happens is that when the document attached to the email is opened, malware is automatically and remotely installed which then subsequently is used to steal data and compromise operations – what is more commonly known as "spear-phishing".

That being said, it is not as simple as just sending an email and waiting for someone to open it, and there are several examples of Palestinian hackers using social engineering where the content and the image of the email is crafted to lure the reader into opening it. In addition, when the email is first opened, there is a clear necessity not to be compromised in order to extract information over a longer period of time.

The best example is the breach of several Israeli government websites, when a number of employees received an email from a non-existent sender with an attachment. As they opened the email, a pornographic video showed up on the screen, at the same time as the malware was installed on the computer system, allowing the sender to extract information from the victim. Trend Micro, working on IT security, simply stated that the use of pornography was a "touch of genius".[35] As the very inappropriate content was opened, the employees would hesitate to report the incident since they did not want to admit having opened up pornography on their work computer. In addition, the receiver of the email was distracted from the actual infection taking place as the content was being played on the screen. Thus, the malware would be quietly ignored and could run for a longer time than usual without being removed. In other words, hackers and hacktivists can be as technologically "savvy" as they can be, but without a dose of cleverness to gain the victim's trust, the intrusion will in most cases be meaningless.

So the necessary question we have to raise is the following: how sophisticated are Gaza Hacker Team and the rest of the Palestinian hackers in terms of the knowledge and development of hacker tools? The answer seems to be, with the information we have at hand: not very much. When analyzing the tools used by the majority of Palestinian hacktivists from Gaza we see that one in particular is recurring: remotely accessed Trojans (RATs).

Essentially, the Trojan is used for espionage, and its convenience lies in the fact that it is controlled directly by humans who can adapt it according to the different defenses they want to penetrate – as was the case with the specific "Xtreme Rat" used against the Israeli police. The tool has historically been so popular with Chinese hackers that it has almost become synonymous with intrusions from China.

However, I have no intention of going into the specifics of the use of RATs; rather I want to point out that the use of this particular kind of malware also seems to have become the preferred tool of several Arab hackers in general and Palestinian hackers in particular. An obvious benefit for Arab and Palestinian hackers is that the use of RATs then also works as a decoy since attention is drawn to a completely different part of the world. As FireEye warned, "off-the-shelf Remote Access Tool (RAT) shouldn't be automatically linked to Chinese threat actors".[36]

What is important to note here is that RATs are publicly or commercially available to anyone who deems them beneficial. Furthermore, they are easy to use.[37] Thus, Gaza Hacker Team and several other Palestinian hackers could, and should, be considered as "script-kiddies" – a pejorative term used for someone unskilled in hacking and dependent on tools developed by others. This stands in contrast to one of the Arab hacktivist teams considered among the most advanced and dangerous, The Desert Falcons, which is believed to have been the first Arab group to develop and launch cyber-espionage operations from scratch.[38]

However, though Gaza Hacker Team and other Palestinian hacktivists use already developed tools, this is not the same as saying that they do not constitute a threat to the Israeli cyber-infrastructure. Just because the tools are already there – either for free or for purchase – does not limit their potential damage. As was written in the report "Security Quality Requirements Engineering", prepared for the US Department of Defense, a script kiddy was described as, "The more immature but unfortunately often just as dangerous exploiter of security lapses on the Internet".[39] Furthermore, as Micro Trend wrote about the cyberattacks on Israel and explicitly stated in regard to the security of Israel:

> Israel is one of the most highly defended countries in
> the world, sheltered behind the legendary "Iron Dome".

But all of that counts for nothing when an attacker –
possibly seeking out revenge for Israeli air strikes on Gaza
last year – circumvents all of that to strike right at the
heart of the Israeli administration. … In fact, for every
Stuxnet, there are hundreds of rather straightforward
spear-phishing campaigns.[40]

Thus, the pejorative term script kiddy only goes as far as being valuable in the sense of hacker ethos, and not in its actual results and achievements. It could be compared to using a gun: the gun does not inflict any less damage simply because the shooter did not manufacture the weapon himself.

In contrast, from the broader activist movement's point of view, the already developed tools for hacking constitute a valuable resource as they enable a larger group of people to participate in operations and campaigns. One could say that the script kiddy is the natural starting point in the career of the hacker. Furthermore, several hacktivist teams even promote the use of already developed tools, as was done by the Middle East Cyber Army (MECA) during OpIsrael 2015 when they shared links to hacking tools for conducting DDoS attacks.[41]

The same has been done by Gaza Hacker Team, which distributed the work of an Egyptian member of the group, BlackRose, who wrote a "how-to-do-SQL[Structured Query Language]-injection"[42] – one of the most common techniques to bypass a web application's authentication. Thus, the information in a database can suddenly be in the hands of someone who should not have entered it in the first place. As written in the preface of BlackRose's book, "Read this book and you will move directly to the professional class".[43]

It is the "open-source" jihad and resistance 2.0.

6

FROM THE NATION TO THE UMMA

"Can I ask you something?" I thought I had figured out the ideology of Gaza Hacker Team, which was a tad naïve I should admit, but it just needed one sentence before the whole thing unraveled and it felt like I was back at the starting point. At this time, mr.leon and I had been talking more or less regularly for six months and, so far, every time I approached him it felt like one step in the wrong direction would make him cut all contact. Of course, mr.leon never said anything impolite or anything that would suggest that would happen but, nevertheless, although he elaborated a bit more on his answers, he seemed suspicious.

"Is there any difference between Jews and Zionists?" I asked as carefully as I could, as if I was afraid to offend him. It took one minute, two minutes, three minutes. Still no answer. Then suddenly, "Of course there is. Judaism is a Semitic religion as with our prophet Moses, peace be upon him. Yet, Zionism is groups and movements that work for the emigration to Palestine and the killings of Palestinians". I wrote slowly, weighing each word before I pushed the send button, "Yeah, I get that, but… I read your book and it struck me as a bit extreme…"

Perhaps I should start from the beginning. At first it seems evident that the main goal of Gaza Hacker Team is strictly nationalist. That is, to liberate Palestine. Yet what emerges from their aforementioned program of principles is something that clearly rejects the notion of the nationalist Palestinian struggle. Instead, what we are being presented with is not only the transnational ideology of Gaza Hacker Team but also that of traditional Salafi jihadism where there is one single sum and substance to legitimize their struggle: political Islam.

Obviously, there is a vast difference between regular political Islam and Salafi jihadism and even within these two currents you will find smaller branches sticking out and forming their own sets of beliefs, practices and organizations. Just think about the obscure traditional movements and divisions we have already: Within the left-revolutionary movement you will find Marxists, Marxist-Leninists, Maoists, Trotskyists and the like. At the other end, you will find Conservatives, Liberal-Conservatives, Libertarian Conservatives and "Progressive" Conservatives. So hang on while we try to untangle this myriad of diverging ideologies that are being expressed within this peculiar hacktivist team from Gaza.

A "SALAFI JIHADI NATIONALISM"?

Although the use of political Islam and the quotations from the Quran are evident through their whole eighty-page program of principles, we should, before we analyze it, understand that it is nevertheless common for other Palestinian groupings that are evidently national-ist. The best known example would be Hamas, which also sees the resistance against the occupation as a form of jihad. Islamic Jihad is another example, where in several cases the other more secular parties in the Palestinian resistance also have religious references in their rhetoric. Thus, in a Palestinian context, there is nothing unusual when Gaza Hacker Team argues for the use of electronic warfare (or rather electronic jihad) religiously, by the use of several verses from the Quran or through one from the hadith. For example, one of the first verses used is the sūrat al-ʿānkabūt (29:69): "And those who strive for us – We will surely guide them to our ways. And indeed, Allah is with the doers of good."[1]

So far, not something that would strike you with great fear. However, there are several factors and ideological stances that clearly distance Gaza Hacker Team's document from the more nationalist-religious Hamas.

First of all, in the chapter on how to be an electronic jihad-ist, several goals are stated that, summed up, explain what websites are to be targeted. Strikingly, Israel is not explicitly mentioned. Rather, Jewish or Zionist websites along with websites of religious groups that "deviate" from what is perceived as true Islam are the main targets. Mainly the websites of Shiites, Sufis, Ibadis, followers of Ash'arism (al-ashāʿira), websites of infidelity (kufr), atheists and "others".[2] Furthermore, it should be noted that Shiites are referred to by the pejorative rāfiḍa – rejecters.

Thus, so far, the targets that Gaza Hacker Team lists are almost exclusively religious. This comes in addition to websites containing singing, music, gambling, witchcraft, astrology and porn-ography, to mention a few. In other words, a clear Salafi notion of conservative Sunni Islam is emerging from the text, with the use of jihad to spread "the correct version". As the team states: "God commands his followers, the monotheists, to gather their forces and opportunities to terrorize the enemy of his religion."[3]

Furthermore, Gaza Hacker Team explicitly states that the goal of electronic jihad is to "spread the religion of Islam and prosely-tization (da'wa) and contribute to publish the different versions of the jihadist websites" and to "defend the Prophet Muhammad, peace be upon him, and defend him and his people, as well as to defend Islam and expose the Zionist, Kharijite and atheist enemies".[4]

Secondly, an important ideological notion distances Gaza Hacker Team from other politico-religious groups such as Hamas: while Hamas uses Islam as a guideline, including the narrative of jihad and the umma, it only does so through a clearly nationalist narra-tive, in order to legitimize the struggle against the occupation and the establishment of an Islamic state in historical Palestine. It is the long-standing conflict between the three historical-political "nation-alisms" in the Middle East: between al-waṭan (the nation state such as Palestine, Syria and Jordan), al-qawmiyya (the pan-Arabic nation comprising the whole Arab world) and al-umma (the Islamic nation).

The notion of how one is supposed to reach unity in the Arab world has traditionally gone roughly along these lines. A series of independent Arab nations side by side, one greater Arab nation or an Islamic umma which encompasses all Muslims, including those outside the Arab world, such as in Iran and Afghanistan. Thus, Hamas is the embodiment of several of the historical and ideological contradictions that exist in the Arab world today. As Hamas states in its charter, "Hamas regards nationalism [al-waṭaniyya] as part and parcel of the religious faith".[5] Al-waṭan, the nation of Palestine, and Islam are by no means dichotomies but are two sides of the same coin.

In the case of Gaza Hacker Team, this notion of nationalism is, however, nonexistent. Rather, although not the same as the nationalist waṭaniyya, the secular notion of al-qawmiyya (pan-Arab nationalism) is rejected as one of the ideologies that are to be targeted online.[6] Instead, there is a narrative of all Muslims standing together through the umma. One example is how one of the main objectives of an electronic jihadist is to "show loyalty to and pride in your religion and umma" and to represent the umma and improve its representation.[7] Of course, so far we should note that this is not a notion monopolized by jihadists and is in itself not extreme.

So, how could Gaza Hacker Team possibly have ideological ties to Salafi jihadism? On the one hand, they struggle to establish the umma. On the other, this is not controversial within the context as has been described. Yet there are notable exceptions and contradictions that complicate the picture of the ideology of Gaza Hacker Team as Salafi jihadist – namely their ideological notion of Israelis as discussed in the introduction to this chapter.

Zone-H collects mirrors of defaced websites; and the material can be studied in detail on its website.[8] For example, there have been instances where Gaza Hacker Team has posted, in a couple of its defacements of Israeli websites, "Khaybar, Khaybar O Jews … the army of Muhammad will return"[9] – a reference to the battle of

Khaybar in year 629 when the army of Prophet Muhammad won over the Jews living at the oasis of Khaybar, which some have used as an anti-Semitic chant to incite the slaughter and mass killings of Jews. However, and this is why the introduction to the chapter is important, when I asked whether there was a difference between Zionists and Jews, mr.leon, who said he was himself the author of the document, replied "Of course". Secondly, the difference between people of Jewish faith and Zionists is not the only seemingly complicated dichotomy that appears in the nodal point between mr.leon's elaborations and what Gaza Hacker Team's form of principles actually declares.

"But rāfiḍa is a dirty word, isn't it?" I was still confused as I had not yet figured out how mr.leon and Gaza Hacker Team's view on Jews and Zionists could be reconciled, and the same applied to their notions on Shiites and their use of the term rāfiḍa. As I asked mr.leon why Shiite websites had to be targeted, he replied "No, no, they are not even mentioned". I dryly commented that, in fact, it was stated on page 8. "No, they [Shiites] are Muslims and our religion is like their religion of Islam". Rather, the divide between them was merely an old one from the time of the caliphate.

And I should be fair, as the term rāfiḍa had been used as a derogatory term against the Shiites, there was a change where the latter appropriated the term and took possession of it. While Sunni Muslims have used it because they believe Shiites are rejecting the legitimate Islamic authority and leadership, Shiites on the other hand have subsequently termed themselves rejecters as a form of pride since they revolted against what they perceive as tyranny.[10]

Then again, there is a difference between subjugated groups appropriating a negatively laden term to turn its meaning into a symbol of pride, as their political, economic and/or social place in a societal hierarchy are emphasized historically, and when, on the other hand, the subjugators are using the very same term. For instance, where certain parts of the Afro-American community have appropriated the so-called "n-word", it would be qualitatively different if say the Republican Party did the same.

Thus, as the discussion continued, mr.leon completely broke away from the document and the notion of electronic jihad to spread Islam. While, on the one hand, mr.leon stated that hacking could be perceived as an electronic sword, on the other hand, he stated that Islam could not be spread by it.[11] In other words, the document states that the websites of Jews, disbelievers and Shiites should be targeted, among several others, in order to spread their version of Islam. Yet there was a clear differentiation between a Zionist and one of Jewish faith, and Shiites were also considered Muslims.

As the discussion centered on the Salafi jihadist group, the Islamic State, he stated that "The Islamic State is an American and Western product to distort the picture of Islam".[12] Indeed, Gaza Hacker Team has an ideology that is closely linked to that of Salafi jihadism and mr.leon, in our discussion, resembles much more closely someone belonging to the Muslim Brotherhood: "Listen, the first word in the Quran is 'read'. Does reading lead to violence?"

As we discussed political Islam we started centering on the Internet as a means to broaden his view of Islam and how he had discovered scholars he would not have been able to learn from without it. You might think he would mention some kind of jihadist scholar as an inspiration, yet it was the Islamic scholars Ahmed Deedat and Yusuf Estes whom he admired.[13] As Deedat was South African and the American Estes converted to Islam from Christianity in 1991, and both can be regarded as conservative preachers and missionaries, they hardly fit the Salafi jihadist current. Rather, they much more resemble that of the Muslim Brotherhood in addition to the Norwegian group Islam Net – which invited Estes to Norway in 2009.

So far, mr.leon would appear as some form of Hydratopyra-nthropos, the man consisting of fire and water, the most contradictory of elements:[14] "For example", he explained "look at Yusuf Estes' history of Islam! Did someone threaten him? Did someone force him? He talks about the time before Islam; about violence, racism and hatred!"

A CONTINUOUS DIVIDE: OPISRAEL, ANONGHOST AND ANONYMOUS ARAB

I was sitting in front of my computer in the middle of night trying to follow the ongoing events of #OpIsrael, an annual operation on 7 April against Israel where hacker teams all over the world are trying to penetrate its cyber-infrastructure in protest against the occupation. Twitter was flowing over with tweets reporting "the latest breaches", credit cards being hacked and websites being brought down. Anonymous Arab was in the front seat with AnonGhost, Middle East Cyber Army (MECA) and the Tunisian hacktivist team al-Fallaga, which proclaimed it was responsible for the campaign, with several other hacktivist groups and individual hackers throwing themselves into the operation. But what is interesting to note here is how the ideological split in Gaza Hacker Team appeared yet again during OpIsrael with the use of propaganda and material from the Islamic State.

One of the most active groups during OpIsrael was without doubt AnonGhost. During the defacement of Israeli websites they manipulated the historical picture of the Red Army soldier on the rooftop in Berlin into that of an Islamic State fighter holding its flag. And this was one of the less grotesque examples.

Several members of AnonGhost, such as the user AnonGhostTeamLegend (@ungku_nazmi), posted a picture of Jihadi John, the man known to have beheaded several hostages including the journalist James Foley, with the caption: "I AM BACK, KUFFAR!" Mauritania Attacker (@OmarKhattab9541), also a member of AnonGhost, and with the profile picture of two Islamic State soldiers on Twitter, hacked several Israeli Facebook accounts where he posted pictures of Jihadi John holding a knife to the camera on the victim's wall, with the caption, "We are coming to kill you O Jews". Furthermore, written over the picture was "This Page Have [sic] Been Hacked By #AnonGhost Team \!/ Death to all Jews :D".

The defacements of Israeli Facebook accounts came only after the hackers had called the operation an "electronic holocaust" – that made several react. For example, the Anonymous-affiliated Twitter user "Anonymous" (@AnonRRD) with over 15.000 followers at the time pleaded, "Please remove the phrase 'electronic holocaust', #OpIsrael does not mean that, our fight is for the Palestinian people".[15] Also, the official Twitter account of OpIsrael (@Op_Israel), reaffirmed this view, declaring, "To clarify, we at this account do not endorse to usage of the word Holocaust. We did not come up with 'Electronic Holocaust.' #OpIsrael".[16]

When I discussed their use of the term "electronic holocaust" with BlackOps, the official spokesperson of Anonymous Arab, he simply dismissed the idea that there was anything extreme about it and rather felt that it strengthened the attack – without being willing to elaborate why. In addition, he stated the same as mr.leon, which was that there is a qualitative difference between a Zionist and a person of Jewish faith:

> There is a huge difference between Zionism and Judaism. Judaism is the religion of the Hebrews, descendants of the sons of the tribe of Jacob, peace be upon him after Moses, and peace be upon him. Zionism [on the other hand] is a political, racist and extremist movement who seeks to establish the Jewish state in Palestine … We are not threatening any Jew outside of the borders of Palestine, but the Zionists inside of Palestine are our target.[17]

As I tried to get BlackOps to elaborate, the correspondence ended abruptly as I asked him about their partner AnonGhost's use of Islamic State propaganda: He simply stopped responding.

My hypothesis at the time regarding why Islamic State propaganda was used, and which I concluded with, was that AnonGhost did everything for the shock factor. Supporting the Islamic State and their brutal campaign was the most provocative statement one could make, and thus was perfect for getting the attention that so many hacktivist teams crave. Yet the affiliations of AnonGhost would be concluded in January 2016 as, in an official AnonGhost-made video uploaded to the Internet Archive, they pledged allegiance (bay'a) to the Islamic State and stated that they would cooperate with the group Caliphate Cyber Army (CCA).[18]

Starting with the common Islamic hymn (nashīd) so often accompanying jihadist propaganda it started by presenting itself as "The Rise of the Caliphate Ghosts"; then followed a montage of different videos of former hacks, videos from the "caliphate" and of wounded children (most likely Palestinians) crying in a hospital, stating:

> We pledge allegiance to the khalifa [caliph] Abu Baker
>
> To listen and obey
>
> In hardship and ease
>
> and we will not oppose the
>
> caliphate unless
>
> we see clear kuffur [infidelity] and deviation,
>
> and judging from shariah.
>
> We make Allah or [sic] guide and a witness to this.

Concluding with "Caliphate Cyber Army/Cyber Caliphate/Ghost Caliphate/We are #one now" with the IS logo in the background. One should, furthermore, note the immense importance Anonymous has had in influencing the global hacker environment (even the jihadist ones), as AnonGhost paraphrased its slogan "We are legion, we do not forgive, we do not forget, expect us" by stating "We are Muslim,

We are many. Beloved Tawheed [monotheism], Defensed Islam, Rule is Shareea [*sic*]".

It is to my knowledge the first time in the history of man that a hacktivist team officially pledged allegiance to a jihadist group, but I predict it will become more common as hacking becomes a normal part of propaganda and warfare.

A NATION IN THE UMMA

So how are these two apparent dichotomies interconnected? Although it would be an impossible task to give a definite conclusion, some issues should be discussed.

The first thing that needs to be pointed out is the different forms of the document and my discussion with mr.leon. While the first is a nameless "form of principles" – written by mr.leon – which represents Gaza Hacker Team and its ideology as a whole to the outside world, mr.leon is personally accountable for what he tells me in a private conversation. In other words, there is a possibility that the two qualitatively different addressees force the consigner to change the rhetoric and message when he brands and represents himself.

On the other hand, on the more ideological level, it is a question of identity versus practice. As the document has clear Salafi jihadi features, it can be perceived as the ideology that the members identify themselves with and a movement that they want to be a part of. The document can also be a tool of self-affirmation and marketing, as they try to brand themselves as the "toughest, strongest and most uncompromising". If the document is addressed to other hackers, then the image of themselves and the rhetoric they use might be designed to persuade others to join them. As professor at the University of Oslo Brynjar Lia points out in his article "The Islamic State (IS) and its Mediatized Barbarism",[19] there is a fierce competition among different groups for media attention – as in the case of the "civil war" between the al-Qaeda leadership and the Islamic State – and that, "new groups clearly tailored their ideological message to please their donors".[20]

This is not to say that Gaza Hacker Team has any donors, and there is nothing that indicates it does; however, a persuasive rhetoric and image of the group gives it legitimacy and a popularity that is much needed when engaging in operations against different groups, organizations and governments.

Although nationalism – as with Israel – is not mentioned in the document, a clear contradiction emerges as we see (in the chapter "The Most Important Israeli Websites Hacked by Gaza Hacker Team") that a majority of what Gaza Hacker Team lists as the most important hacked websites are in fact Israeli. As they mention hundreds of Israeli websites that have been hacked, only three examples provided fit with the narrative of Gaza Hacker Team as hackers for Islam.

One example of how mr.leon attempted to merge the document's narrative of the umma, the Salafi jihadist features and the nationalist practices (by predominantly hacking Israeli websites), is the use of Ibn Khattab in the Gaza Hacker Team. Ibn Khattab (Thāmir Ṣāliḥ ʿAbdallāh al-Suwaylim), the Saudi Arabian who made a name for himself in the Tajikistan civil war, and then became a military commander in the First and Second Chechen War, has become an important symbol in Salafi jihadism – on a par with Usama Bin Laden and Abu Musab al-Zarqawi. Helped by his good looks and an almost Che Guevara style, and his sensational videos from Chechnya showing the armed attacks on Russian forces, Ibn Khattab would become a living (and later dead) legend and one of the most important symbols for classical jihadism.[21] When mr.leon was asked why one of its members, the hacker TKL, used Ibn Khattab as his personal avatar, he replied:

> The umma must be like one body and structure. If there is
> an attack on one part of the state, the people of the occupied
> city will resist and defend. If they are not able to stop the
> occupation, then there is an obligation for the whole umma to
> resist with them and support them in their war.[22]

Thus mr.leon, with the example of Ibn Khattab, dismissed the dichotomy of fighting for the umma and the nationalist struggle for the liberation of Palestine. The waṭanī perspective and the struggle to defend the umma were not mutually exclusive. Rather, the former constituted a part of the latter.

Yet this goes only as far as mr.leon being a sole representative of Gaza Hacker Team. Another of the three members of the group's leadership, Casper, shows that this ideological contradiction is not only represented in the team as a whole but within the leadership itself.

For example, mr.leon stated that the Islamic State was an American and Western construct to tarnish the image of Islam and in general seems to fit in with the ideology of the Muslim Brotherhood.

However, at the same time we see – if we research the forum of Gaza Hacker Team – that Casper more coherently follows the ideology of the group's document.

The best example is his signature that follows all of his posts in the forum, which consists of a quotation from Abdallah Azzam.[23] Being both a teacher and mentor for Usama Bin Laden, Azzam developed a theory of jihad where his idea of one hour in the path of jihad being worth more than seventy years of praying at home has had great influence on the global jihadist movement. This is an ideological line that recurs in several of Casper's posts on the forum.

Another example is a post from 1 November 2011 when he links to a speech made by the Islamic State's official spokesperson, Abu Muhammad al-Adnani, and refers to him as the jihadist sheikh, shaykh al-mujāhid.[24] Furthermore, in another post, Casper links to several speeches made by Abu Hamza al-Muhajir (also named Abu Ayyub al-Masri), who was the former apocalyptic senior aide of the leader of al-Qaeda in Iraq, Abu Musab al-Zarqawi, before becoming the de facto leader of the Islamic State in Iraq.[25] Several other examples could be mentioned, but my point is to show that there is no uniform ideology within the leadership of Gaza Hacker Team.

As mr.leon seemingly began to get fed up with all my questions for that time, I asked about his and Casper's differing ideologies. He dryly stated: "There is freedom of opinions on the forum and there are differences in opinion on every issue."[26]

Thus it is possible to argue that the organizational structure resembles that of Anonymous, without any comparison otherwise, as hackers from the whole political and ideological spectrum unite through Gaza Hacker Team's means and goals. Gabriella Coleman, in her research on Anonymous, argues that the use of and necessity for pseudonyms and avatars online helps cultivate a functioning cosmopolitanism:

> By cloaking markers of the self, like ethnicity, class and age, all sorts of different possibilities are opened up. Studies confirm that we tend to seek those who are familiar (or similar to us) – and fellowship via shared identity is nothing to scoff at, nor eliminate. Nevertheless, it is also important to create and experiment with spaces that mute markers of class, age, and background to help form connections that might not otherwise be made.[27]

Then it is perhaps not too surprising that the members and forum participants are united by what seems to be their common denominator, Islam – or rather political Islam.

THE SECULAR GOALS OF AL-MUJĀHID AL-ILIKTRŪNĪ

The different ideological contradictions of Gaza Hacker Team have been discussed within the framework of religion and resistance, but we should still focus some more on the religious Salafi jihadist superstructure.

This time we focus on their representation of themselves on their homepage/forum where there is the same underlining of a *religious* battle rather than a secular resistance. For example, they choose not to employ the secular term "electronic resistance" (al-muqāwama al-iliktrūniyya), but rather use "electronic jihad" (al-jihād al-iliktrūnī). Furthermore, the members of that forum constitute the Islamic Network (al-shabaka al-islāmiyya) – the same as in their document.

The forum does not only limit itself to discussing matters such as security, already conducted and future hacks, or technical issues, but there is also a separate forum for Islamic issues (al-aqsām al-islāmiyya).[28]

One example, with several Israeli websites hacked in August 2012, were the defacements with the introduction of religious verses and "In the name of God, the lord of the jihadists and martyrs" (bismillāh rabb al-mujāhidīn wa al-shuhadā') and the sūrat al-tawba (9:14).[29] By combining these texts, as in July 2012, with pictures of masked men holding a black flag with the Islamic profession of faith (al-shahāda),[30] commonly used by other jihadist groups such as Jabhat al-Nuṣra and the Islamic State,[31] they seemingly attempt to create a narrative of a politico-religious battle for the liberation of Palestine; an attempt to establish a narrative of themselves not just as armed fighters, but as holy cyber-warriors.

There are substantial numbers of additional examples that could be given, but what is interesting is to compare the form of the defacements with the actual content: the goals and demands of the hacktivist group. If we interpret the content in a political context where Gaza Hacker Team are not dismissed as mere terrorists or fanatics, it becomes apparent that a substantial majority of their goals and demands are in fact secular-nationalist and tactical, as is the case with Hamas. The example given, with the use of sūrat al-tawba and God as the lord of the jihadists and martyrs, to show the jihadist narrative of Gaza Hacker Team was in fact a protest to stop the violations of holy sites in Palestine. Other examples are protests against the death of Arafat Jaradat during imprisonment in Israel in 2013,[32] solidarity with and protest against the treatment of Palestinian prisoners on hunger strike – and with Palestinian Islamic Jihad member Khaḍr ʿAdnān in particular[33] – or as a protest against Operation Pillar of Defense in Gaza in 2012.[34]

Obviously, these examples do contain shades of grey as regards actual secularism – especially when it comes to the demand to stop the violations of holy places. Some would argue, and rightly so, that it constitutes a religious aspect that transcends the national borders of Palestine, at the same time as it should be considered a demand that cuts across ordinary religious dividing lines. For example, although the al-Aqsa mosque is a holy site for Muslims, it is hard to believe that secular and Christian Palestinians would be indifferent to the issue. Yet these demands and the goals they set for themselves when they send a message to the Israelis are strongly Palestinian nationalist.

As documented earlier by other scholars, this phenomenon of Islamist groups with secular-nationalist goals is nothing new and rather more normal than one might think. One example – with no comparison otherwise – is Hamas and Islamic Jihad which justify their jihad in religious terms, but only to reach what can be termed secular-nationalist goals. As Robert Pape states in his study of every suicide attack from 1980 until 2005:

Examinations of these crucial cases [Islamic Jihad and Hamas' suicide bombing campaigns in the 1990s] demonstrates that the terrorist groups came to the conclusion that suicide attacks accelerated Israel's withdrawal in both cases. Although the Oslo Accords formally committed Israel to withdrawing the IDF from Gaza and the West Bank, Israel routinely missed key deadlines, often by many months, and the terrorists came to believe that Israel would not have withdrawn when it did, and perhaps would not have withdrawn at all, but for the coercive leverage of suicide attacks.[35]

Furthermore, Pape emphasizes that:

Rather, what nearly all suicide terrorist attacks have in common is a specific secular and strategic goal: to compel modern democracies to withdraw military forces from territory that the terrorists consider their homeland. Religion is rarely the root cause, although it is often used as a tool by terrorist organizations in recruiting and in other efforts in service of the broader strategic objective.[36]

Thus, although there is anti-Semitism in the Palestinian territories, it does not give a satisfactory explanation for the attacks on Israel. This is something confirmed by Gaza Hacker Team when, in a common message during defacements, it was emphasized that "The war continues until the last Zionist on the land of beloved Palestine".[37] As already mentioned, the group, or at least mr.leon, believes that there is in fact a difference between Zionists and people of Jewish faith and thus the message does not necessarily imply the expelling of Israeli Jews.

The same implicit distinction between Jews and Zionists was also made in the YouTube video labeled "A Message to the Zionist Enemy",[38] where there was no mention of Jewish responsibility, the Jewish state or anything similar, but rather the "Zionist enemy", "Zionist Israeli sites" were singled out and it was the Israeli government and parliament, the Knesset, that were threatened with being hacked. Also, this time the threat had an explicit nationalist-secular demand: the end of the brutal treatment of Samir Issawi and that nothing was to be done against him.[39]

Even if we take their name, Gaza Hacker Team (Farīq Qarāṣinat Ghazza), into consideration, there is nothing particularly jihadist about it at all. For instance, the majority of Salafi jihadist groups explicitly state their politico-religious affiliations and adherence through their names, such as the group of Abu Musab al-Zarqawi, Jamā'at al-Tawḥīd wa al-Jihād (The Group of Monotheism and Jihad), or Anṣār al-Sunna, another Iraqi insurgent group – where the first word "anṣār" (supporters) has a clear link to the supporters of the Prophet Muhammad who helped him escape from Mecca when he faced persecution.

Usama Bin Laden was, for that very same reason, annoyed when Western media shortened the full name of his organization Qā'idat al-Jihād ("The Base of Jihad") to al-Qaeda, because the simple word "base" alone did not have anything to do with Islam.[40] By virtue of its name, Gaza Hacker Team seems to identify more strongly with the hacker ethos than with that of Salafi jihadism.

Even so, an important exception has to be mentioned. The secular goals of the Gaza Hacker Team only go as far as resisting the occupation and attacking Israeli websites. However, as mentioned, there have been occasions when they have extended their paradigm of resisting from the notion of al-waṭan, to the notion of the umma, the Islamic nation transcending the borders of the former. This was stressed at the beginning of the interviews with Gaza Hacker Team when they explicitly stated that they did not limit their hacktivism to the Israelis and that their targets were "Zionist websites, those who are against our Islam and the atheist websites".[41]

An example of the latter is the attack on Uganda's Ministry of Education and Sports website, among others, in 2012, when neither the Israeli occupation nor the blockade of Gaza was mentioned. The defacement was rather done to show what they termed "the real message of Islam" and to express solidarity with "Muslim brothers oppressed politically", with links to several Islamic websites such as The Key to Islam and Islam Way.[42] Again, these Islamic websites do not represent the same ideology as Salafi jihadism, but closely resemble that which would be common in groups ideologically linked with the Muslim Brotherhood.[43]

Another example was the hacked website of Burma's Ministry of Information during the 2012 Rakhine State riots – a conflict mainly between Rakhine Buddhists and Rohingya Muslims, with several killed – which also resulted in arbitrary arrests, killings and segregation of the Rohingya following decades of discrimination against the Muslim minority.[44] It made the Gaza Hacker Team declare that the government site was hacked as a protest against "your crimes against Muslims in Borma [*sic*]" and demanding "Freedom for Muslims in Borma [*sic*]".[45] If the persecution did not end, Gaza Hacker Team stated, the Burmese would pay with their lives, illustrated with a screenshot from an al-Qaeda video.

Again, we see a team where ideological contradictions emerge from politically moderate Islam to Salafi jihadism. However, out of the hacked websites, and turning back to the initial analysis of Gaza Hacker Team, these two examples do constitute two exceptions and the overall picture of the group is of a hacktivist team with secular-nationalist goals and demands: the end of the Israeli occupation and the killing of Palestinians.

Thus, the problem in defining Gaza Hacker Team ideologically might lie in the use of categories that are too strict. Islamism – from the moderate to the extreme sides of the ideology with the division between violent/non-violent – is a clearly hybrid phenomenon and, as Thomas Hegghammer, director of terrorism research at the Norwegian Defense Research Establishment, has emphasized regarding the problems in coherently conceptualizing Salafi jihadism:

> First, it is very difficult to operationalise the notion of radicalism or intransigence. At which level of extremism does an actor start to cease to be a Jihadi-Salafi? ... Second, it is not at all clear how operational the Salafi-*ikhwani* [Muslim Brotherhood] dichotomy is in the world of contemporary militant Islamism.[46]

Rather, the diverging notions, expressions and contradictions of Gaza Hacker Team and the categories to describe them must not be seen as isolated boxes where they only fit in one of them, but rather as overlapping structures.[47] For example, the fact that Gaza Hacker Team wants to use the sword to spread Islam tells us just as little as Western political parties' goals of creating "a better world" about their actual political preferences.[48] That is, Gaza Hacker Team's Islamist slogans are in many senses too vague to tell us anything about the expected political behavior of the group in the short and medium term.

7

ISLAMIC JIHAD AND HAMAS: THE PALESTINIAN CYBER-BRIGADES

Offering me tea and food while they looked through my passport, the conversation with Hamas was in the beginning more about where I came from, where I lived and what I was doing in Norway than about Palestinian hacktivism. If I had known then what I know now, the irony would not have been lost upon me. Perhaps the Norwegian National Security Authority (NNSA) could learn something from Hamas when it came to public relations and being pleasant, in spite of the need for "security".

HAMAS: "NECESSITY IS THE MOTHER OF INVENTIONS"

The popular resistance has existed for 25 years with the intifada, and we have not accomplished anything because of the Jews. We, the popular resistance, throw stones at them and they throw tear gas at us and so on. 30 minutes of demonstration and then we will leave.[1]

The two Hamas members I met were somewhat disillusioned with the methods of the popular resistance, as illustrated by the above quotation. Nevertheless, they said they supported every aspect of the resistance that harmed the occupation, including the latest string of attacks in Jerusalem in the autumn of 2013 – although they distanced themselves from the killing of children and civilians. Their support for the Palestinian resistance also included the aspect of electronic warfare.

In the ḥamsāwīs' view we live in a world where there is a continuous technological development with the establishment of digital bank accounts, public information, media and modern psychological warfare – and thus the resistance had to keep pace, bringing itself into the virtual realm. As one of the Hamas members stated, "Necessity is the mother of inventions".[2] The litmus test, the categorical imperative as such, was whether the actions of the resistance hurt the occupation and the Israeli state.

This support for every part of the resistance was also applied to the electronic resistance as the possibility was perceived of damaging the Israeli state economically by hacking bank accounts, weakening the occupation's narrative through a media war or even directly, however hypothetically, through war and hacking Israel's weapons (the hacking of rockets was used as an example).

There was in addition, according to the interviewees, several advantages to the electronic resistance such as avoiding being confronted, hurt or killed by Israeli soldiers – in contrast to armed operations and demonstrations. However, the aspect of materiality (the "real world") was apparent. This was in addition combined with the notion of martyrdom operations ('amaliyyāt istishhādiyya):

How do you want to liberate yourself? It is correct, you liberate yourself by blood, and you liberate yourself by sacrifices. How do you want to get rid of this wall, this checkpoint? It has to be sacrifices by blood, sacrifices by money and soul until you get rid of this checkpoint, this occupation and so on. So the electronic ways … while you're sitting at home by yourself … but at the same time I'm on the ground and I have to resist with my body since this is the reality which we live in.[3]

Turning to the empirical data and the specific examples of the hacking and counter-hacking between Hamas and Israel, we can state that although it can be branded as a cyberwar, there are nevertheless those hacks that involve a bit of dark humor. For example, in March 2001, the website of Hamas was hacked so visitors of the website were diverted to "Hot Motel Horny Sex Sluts" instead – a website few would suspect the regular Hamas supporter would enjoy.

Ahmad Yassin, then-leader of Hamas before being killed by the occupation forces in his wheelchair in 2004, was not too happy about it and stated that they would use any means available, including through the Internet, to wage jihad against Israel.[4] History was going to prove him right. According to an anonymous Palestinian security official in 2015:

Gaza security agencies succeeded in uncovering the identities of dozens of spies recruited by Israeli intelligence through a specific website. This was accomplished when Palestinian technology experts penetrated the servers of an Israeli security agency and retrieved the list of agents kept there.[5]

The Palestinian security official confirmed what everyone knew: Hamas has developed electronic defense units including hackers within the movement. This is hardly surprising considering that Israel not only has several capable hackers in its ranks but also uses social media, Internet monitoring and the like to identify vulnerable Palestinians in order to make them collaborators.

You do not even have to be that vulnerable, only reckless in your use of it, as was proved in 2014 when Israel assassinated one of the leaders of Hamas' military wing, Hamza Abū al-Hayjāʾ, after finding his location through his personal Facebook account.[6] If the dangers of Facebook were pointed out in the introduction, this is definitely on another level in the occupied territories.

What we should note is that every time there is a confrontation on the ground between the Palestinians and the Israelis, there is a naturally corresponding intensification online. As with the bombings of Gaza in 2008/2009, 2012 and 2014 or with the uprisings in Jerusalem, Israel sees an increase in cyberattacks both from within and abroad. For example, the hacker "Cold Zero" hacked 2,000 Israeli websites alone, 800 of them during the 2008 massacre in Gaza – amongst them the website of the Israeli political party Likud. When he was arrested by Israeli authorities, he was found to be a seventeen-year-old Palestinian "Israeli-Arab" citizen. Furthermore, the pro-Hamas hacker "Nimu al-Iraq" modified the DDoS tool al-Durrah especially for the events of 2008.[7]

Of course, these forms of hacking and counter-hacking operations between Hamas and its supporters and Israel could be described ad infinitum. Paulo Shakarian, Jana Shakarian and Andrew Ruef rightly attribute the attacks to the intensifying media war between the Palestinians and Israel, as the attacks are not limited to being just a tool but are a part of influencing the media narrative.[8]

As Gaza is under total blockade, hidden behind great walls and with a sea embargo imposed on it, unable to bother any of the Israelis living their daily lives on the other side, the media war and hacking of Israeli sites are the embodiment of "Like it or not, we're here, no matter how much you pretend not to see us".[9]

ISLAMIC JIHAD: THE ELECTRONIC JIHAD WILL NOT BE TELEVISED

As I prepared the fieldwork for this book, it was never my intent to discuss the issue of electronic jihad with Palestinian Islamic Jihad. While there were several articles on the hackers in Hamas, there were far fewer articles about the cyberattacks of Islamic Jihad. Nevertheless, Islamic Jihad has an electronic unit in the Sarāyā al-Quds, the Jerusalem Brigade, which has existed since 2008 according to the news site Menassat which covers the Middle East and North Africa.[10] But they did not seem to matter to the same extent as the Hamas hackers.

However, as we discussed the hackers in the Izz al-Din al-Qassam Brigade, the two members of Hamas several times changed the subject to the hackers of Islamic Jihad – most likely because of their unwillingness to discuss the inner structures and tactics of their own movement. It did, to say the least, pique my curiosity.

The main representative of Islamic Jihad was a calm, friendly and pious man. He did not smoke because of his religious convictions and tried to scale down his intake of coffee for the same reason.

As we talked about Islamic Jihad and its involvement in electronic jihad, he put forward many of the same ideas that were held by Hamas, and primarily the notion that any kind of resistance to the occupation not only should be, but must be supported. As with Hamas, he emphasized that the technological innovations had forced them to implement changes in order to keep pace with the Israelis, as they were more technologically advanced. Thus, the "first steps" had been taken to "accelerate the end of the occupation" and he confirmed that there was "a specialized unit which is a part of the al-Quds brigade which belongs to the military jihad, there is a part with the political jihad and then there are the civil entities that practice their work to a great extent in the Gaza Strip".[11]

He summed up the goals of the electronic war, as he phrased it, in three main points:

1. Prevent electronic attacks from Israel.
2. Prevent espionage and surveillance.
3. Spread the Palestinian cause to the rest of the world and international media.

The two first points (preventing electronic attacks, espionage and surveillance) indicate the main needs of the Islamic Jihad movement as being of a defensive nature. Thus, he broke with the Gaza Hacker Team and Hamas narrative of hacktivism and electronic resistance as a mainly offensive tool in order to conduct attacks on the Israeli cyber-infrastructure. Rather, electronic jihad was a necessity in making the organization and its armed brigade work more effectively and safely, "Especially, in its tracing, monitoring and jamming operations as for example jamming the monitoring of phone lines".

However, the tasks of the electronic brigade in Islamic Jihad were not limited to these defensive measures, but were in addition to the more offensive operations against the Israeli cyber-infrastructure. He used the al-Quds Brigade's hacking of an Israeli government website where Islamic Jihad obtained the email addresses of 20,000 Israeli soldiers as an example. Following the hack, the Israeli soldiers received threatening emails – a typical feature of psychological warfare used to instill fear and named by the al-Quds Brigade as a War of Nerves.[12] It should be mentioned that 20,000 is a particularly high number, but most likely he referred to Islamic Jihad's counter-cyberattack during Israel's Operation Pillar of Defense on 17 November 2012 – at that the time newest offensive against the population in the Gaza Strip.

If we are to believe the news articles on Islamic Jihad's hacking of the Israeli government website, the number was "limited" to 5,000 affected Israeli soldiers. As a result of the hack, they received an email with the message "Gaza will be the graveyard of your soldiers and Tel Aviv will be a ball of fire", written in Hebrew.[13]

On 19 November, two days after the War of Nerves hacking, an Israeli air strike hit a fifteen-story office building in Gaza City. One of the militants in the building, Ramez Harb, who was the head of Islamic Jihad's media operations, and according to Israel responsible for the propaganda efforts, was killed instantly.[14] Four years earlier, in 2008, Islamic Jihad took responsibility for several hacked and defaced Israeli websites in the wake of the killing of Hassan Ziyad Shaqura, the former head of the movement's media branch. Thus, there should be no doubt that Israel deems the propaganda measures of the Palestinian groups as a threat.

That is not to say that a War of Nerves always works out as planned, which Hamas, or at least Hamas sympathizers, painfully experienced in 2014 during Operation Protective Edge – the bombing of Gaza during the summer of 2014. As someone logged on to visit the Facebook page of Domino's Pizza Israel, it was not the usual content that was showing. Instead, for approximately an hour, the header was changed to a picture of a Palestinian militant with the text "The Qassam Brigade//Electronic wing". Furthermore, the status updates for Domino's Israel did not say anything about pizza but "Today we will strike deep in Israel, Tel Aviv, Haifa, Jerusalem, Ashkelon, Ashdod more than 2000 rockets. We'll start at 7. Counting back towards the end of Israel. Be warned!"[15]

It was, in other words, supposed to be a menacing message that would plant fear in the hearts of Israelis. But, as we so often experience in our lives, things do not always turn out as planned. The hackers were instead ridiculed and mocked by the Israeli visitors, as the situation developed into a competition to write the funniest comeback.

One Facebook user's response was, for example, "Hey, please reserve a missile for me with jalapenos, green olives, extra cheese, and mushrooms. You have my address. Tell the delivery boy to activate the alarm when it is arriving, so I know to put my pants on".[16]

When the hackers published a photo of Israelis taking cover in a sewer pipe with the caption "The right place for every Israel [*sic*] – the sewer pipe, hahaha!", an Israeli replied, "You know who lives in sewers? And what they eat?", posting a picture of the Super Mutant Ninja Turtles eating pizza.[17]

Not too many Israelis seemed to be scared.

But to continue on the issue of the Islamic Jihad hackers: interestingly, the main representative of the group refuted the notion that the Islamic Jihad hackers were a relatively new phenomenon, only existing since 2008 according to Menassat. He emphasized that the work had been going on since 1999, when – after a political decree from the movement's leadership – a process of incorporating the electronic brigade into the al-Quds Brigade and Islamic Jihad had begun which had "evolved significantly" since then. However, as the main representative was emphasizing the use of the hackers to prevent wire-tapping and spying operations by the occupation forces, it is possible that although the offensive operations are relatively new, the preventive electronic measures have existed in the movement for more than ten years.

In addition, the main representative of Islamic Jihad stated that its hackers did not necessarily go public with all of their attacks. For them, the importance was to win military and strategic victories and not to get media publicity: "We work in silence and in calm in order to achieve our goals and defeat the occupation."[18] Thus, the revolution is apparently not the only thing not being televised, to paraphrase Gil Scott-Heron.[19]

IMPORTING ELECTRONIC JIHAD

It is important, and equally interesting, that the members of Hamas stated that they had got help from abroad in developing the cyber-warriors of the Izz al-Din al-Qassam Brigade: "We don't deny that some countries helped us with this, do you understand?";[20] and when asked whether the situation was any different for Islamic Jihad, the main representative of the Islamic Jihad movement stated:

> No, of course, this army has gotten help, education and
> training from different agencies that support the Palestinian
> cause. There are both local and foreign specialties in this field.
> We all aim for the same goal and we have received modern
> hardware [devices] through different agencies who are friends
> of the Palestinian people and there are also parts bought
> from the local and the black market in order to continue
> our development.[21]

Not too surprisingly, when he was asked if the help came from Iran, he stated bluntly that he did not have "enough information" on the subject.

However, it is not farfetched to highlight the work of Iran when it comes to the development of cyber-brigades in the Arab world – among others, because of their close ideological links – since the main representative of Islamic Jihad considered the Iranian revolution and Khomeini an inspiration for the movement.

As Abu Ahmad, the spokesperson of the armed al-Quds Brigade, stated, according to al-Monitor: "We are not the only Palestinian armed group that receives Iranian support, but we are the one that admits it the loudest. We feel it's like an inevitable gratitude."[22] This is in addition to the knowledge we have today of Iran as one of the foremost countries regarding cyber-technology (often mentioned alongside Russia and China), and Iran is described by the Institute for National Security Studies as one of the "most active players in the international cyber arena".[23]

In his book *The War Against the People*, the Israeli peace activist Jeff Halper asks how Israel possibly can get away "with it all". Many blame the Israeli lobby American Israel Public Affairs Committee (AIPAC), but we tend to forget about the American arms lobby; companies such as Northrop Grumman, Lockheed Martin and the rest of the war profiteers certainly surpass the AIPAC when it comes to funding American politicians.[24] Israel has been in constant conflict since its establishment, with four conventional wars and seven asymmetrical or unconventional wars,[25] and it has simultaneously needed to pacify the Palestinians, taking the perspective that the occupation will never end. The Israeli occupation can in many respects be compared to the "War on Terror": does anyone really believe it will ever be won?

Yet when it comes to pacifying the Palestinians, it is also a perfect testing ground for weapons – what Halper terms the "Laboratory" of Palestinians. For example, one of the leading arguments of the Israeli arms industry is that the weapons have been tested under "realistic environments"; it is in addition immensely important for American arms producers as it is also a laboratory for American arms and equipment. For example, during Operation Protective Edge in Gaza the IDF employed and tested the HTR 2000, a sniper rifle produced by H-S Precision in the United States.[26] As the former Israeli Defense Minister Benjamin Ben Eliezer explained, "People like to buy things that have been tested. If Israel sells weapons, they have been tested, tried out. We can say we've used this 10 years, 15 years".[27]

On the other hand, this also works the other way around, including in respect of the cyber-capabilities of Hamas and other Palestinian groupings in Gaza. As there is an ongoing struggle among the Arab states to attain regional hegemony and dominance, and in particular between the Gulf States themselves and against Iran, Gaza is also a laboratory for their products. According to Aviad Dadon from the AdoreGroup, Qatar has invested millions in the defensive and offensive cyber-capabilities used in Gaza. Not only that, according to the same source they have also trained several members of Hamas in how to use "sophisticated" equipment such as modern camera systems in Hamas' tunnel system.[28]

Of course, as Henry Kissinger once said, America does not have permanent friends nor enemies, it has interests, and the cooperation between Qatar and Hamas is no different.[29] In fact, since Qatar perceives Saudi Arabia as a threat, it uses Gaza as a proving ground to ensure that its investment in the cyber-infrastructure has paid off: "They are taking lessons from the performance of their cyber-equipment and will improve them even further for the next war, which will be even more cyber-oriented than this one."[30]

The claim that Qatar is sponsoring Hamas adds up to the allegations of money and equipment transfers from, among others,

Iran, Turkey and, ironically, Saudi Arabia. Thus, it is reasonable to believe that Islamic Jihad and Hamas have received state support to develop their hacker capabilities, as they have received the same state support for other technological areas.

However, so far in this book I have not mentioned a single Palestinian hacktivist team or electronic warfare unit residing in the West Bank. Why is that the case, and what is so special about Gaza when it comes to electronic jihad?

WHY GAZA?

With names such as Gaza Hacker Team, or with the recent revelation that the members of the KDMS Team, about which we will learn later on in this book, are residents of Gaza,[31] everything indicates that the majority of Palestinian hacktivist teams, and the hackers of Hamas and Islamic Jihad for that matter, live and work in the Gaza Strip while there are no known teams from the West Bank. This lack of hacktivist teams or operations from the West Bank was confirmed by mr.leon, who stated that "There are no teams from the West Bank" and that the only team that ever existed was the so-called "Ghaḍab Falasṭīn" (The anger of Palestine), whose members quit in order to pursue their social lives.[32]

So how did it happen that hacktivist teams and hacktivist operations apparently flourish in Gaza, while there are no well-known or effective hacktivist teams in the West Bank? The explanation might lie in the fact that the situation in the West Bank and the Gaza Strip is completely different. Not only in terms of living conditions, work and education but also, and mainly, through the qualitatively different *means of control* employed by the Israelis.

With the Gaza Strip under blockade, with a strict control on goods going in and out, drones and numerous bombings, mr.leon stressed that there were several difficulties – especially during Operation Protective Edge, in the summer of 2014, when #OpSaveGaza was launched: power outages, a slow or non-functioning Internet, damaged or outdated hardware, in addition to the fact that, as mentioned, several of the members' homes were bombed. This led him to admit that "our attacks were really weak this summer".[33] Thus, one might easily assume that the Gaza Strip would be the least suitable place to pursue hacktivism or electronic resistance, unlike the situation in the West Bank, where the tension level might be higher, but there is better access to a more stable Internet connection and to electricity.

There is, on the other hand, one important factor that might be decisive: there are no Israeli soldiers present on the ground in Gaza conducting raids and arrests – with the exception of extraordinary events such as during escalations. The West Bank might have less control imposed on movement – to a certain degree and depending on focus – but is also far more troubled by daily arrests, nightly raids in Palestinian villages and demolitions of Palestinian homes. In addition, one has to take the constant surveillance of Palestinians' phones and computers into consideration, where most aspects of your life might be used against you:

> In testimonies and interviews given to the media, they [forty-three veterans from the Israeli military unit "Unit 8200"]

specified that data were gathered on Palestinians' sexual orientations, infidelities, money problems, family medical conditions and other private matters that could be used to coerce Palestinians into becoming collaborators or create divisions in their society.[34]

With this at the back of the minds of the Palestinians in the West Bank, it might lead to self-limitations in the field of resistance – with all of the consequences they might face because of their actions. Thus, the opportunities for conducting hacktivism might be fewer, contrary to the situation in the Gaza Strip where – despite the blockade – residents might feel safe from Israeli soldiers bursting through their doors.

This is a hypothesis that was confirmed by the main representative of Palestinian Islamic Jihad in the West Bank as he – independently from the other sources – verified that there were no Palestinian hackers outside Gaza. Furthermore, he explained the uneven development as being a result of what he labeled a "direct" occupation of the West Bank and thus implicitly the "indirect" occupation of Gaza, as the latter was more suitable for pursuing electronic resistance – especially regarding Israeli control of the infrastructure such as phone lines, ISPs and network companies.

Moreover, he pointed out another decisive factor: the role of the Palestinian Authority's cooperation with the Israelis on security issues, where those stepping out of line were imprisoned, turned over to the Israeli military or, even worse, tortured or killed. This notion is plausible as the representatives of Hamas and the Stop the Wall

Campaign also considered – to a certain degree – the PA as a greater threat to the resistance than the Israeli forces themselves.

This led the representative of Islamic Jihad to claim that:

> These three considerations have led to a state of no hackers in the existing or required form on the West Bank. There are only web-surfers, but no specialists in this field. However, there have appeared some names that have a role, but they are not organized and worked individually when they attacked the networks and the Israeli websites. In fact, I was in prison with one of them.[35]

It is not just the security cooperation between the Palestinian Authority and the Israeli occupation forces that should be taken into consideration. The Hamas government simply does not exist when it comes to combating cybercrime. That makes room not just for politically motivated electronic resistance but also for the rather more malicious Palestinian cybercrime, among others.

For example, with the blockade of Gaza and the isolation caused by it, a Palestinian programmer broke into the phone network to call his family outside Palestine for free.[36] Thus he did what *phreaks* (combining freaks and the prefix ph-, as in phone) were already doing in the US in the late 1950s as they managed to recreate the tones of the telephone system used to route long-distance calls and thus make free calls. One of them, I should mention, was Steve Jobs.

The situation in Gaza is so absurd, for lack of a better word, that a Palestinian student in Algeria who became involved in professional hacking was prosecuted by the Algerian authorities. Returning to his home in Rafah, he was finally safe, since Palestinian law enforcement, with Palestinian law dating back to 1936, had not caught up with the technology.[37]

However, we should not dismiss the judicial situation in Gaza as being because of "backward" Arabs, since the Philippine government found itself in exactly the same situation in 2000 with regard to the ILOVEYOU computer worm that caused over $15 billion in damage.[38] There were no laws in the Philippines against writing malware at the time, so those responsible, Reonel Ramones and Onel de Guzman, were released, with all charges against them dropped.

The politically motivated Palestinian hackers and the cyber-criminals in Gaza are not necessarily two distinct groups. Rather, they appear to overlap. As Islām Shahwān, the spokesman for the Ministry of Interior in Gaza, stated on the issue of cybercrime: the Palestinian hackers who conduct credit card fraud and other illegal schemes have a good reputation in the Gaza Strip, as they not only use their knowledge to enrich themselves, but also work against the Israeli occupation, and therefore form part of the resistance.[39]

Thus, the hackers of Gaza interestingly embody Eric Hobsbawm's thesis of "the social bandit", the man robbing and plundering, yet rendered by the common people as a hero and part of the resistance.[40] Are then the hackers from Gaza the modern Palestinian version of the Mexican revolutionary Pancho Villa or the Hungarian outlaw Sándor Rózsa?

Gaza may seem like a haven for hackers, but measures have been taken and Palestinian hackers in Gaza stated themselves that there was a risk of being arrested by the Hamas government. Not because of the hacking itself, but, they explained, when a website affiliated with the government was hacked or taken down, they were the ones suspected. Hamas, on the other hand, denied the allegations and stated that it supported the Palestinian hacktivists' operations against Israel.[41]

Gaza Hacker Team did, however, give an important explanation when they were asked about the issue of hacktivism (or rather the lack of it) in the West Bank: "We generally help all the Arab hackers through lessons and courses to develop their hacking skills, and the development of new methods."[42] Thus, although we cannot be certain, we might, on the one hand, have seen a development where the lack of Palestinian hacktivists in the West Bank has caused it to remain so. On the other hand, the presence of Palestinian hacktivists in the Gaza Strip might have led to a rise of the phenomenon, with several independent and active teams.

As a student who graduated from the Islamic University of Gaza said when he was interviewed by al-Monitor:

> I no longer like to directly work in hacking calls ... I prefer working on developing programs that facilitate the hacking process, then selling them to hackers in Gaza. The prices of the hacking software differs [*sic*] for each client, depending on their ability [to pay] as well as the nature of the software.[43]

This does additionally strengthen the hypothesis of several of the Gaza hackers being script-kiddies.

It is necessary to comment on the story of Gaza as a safe haven for Palestinian hacktivists. It is possible that the Gaza Strip only has the role of a potential "honeypot"[44] – the metaphor referring to the bear attracted to and stealing honey. This means that there might be hackers residing in Gaza, but not necessarily constituting the hot-spot. However, the honeypot lures the attention of potential threats, such as the Israeli hackers or intelligence services, away from the "real" hacktivists. Although this possibility cannot be excluded, it is highly unlikely as every single source, including hackers, Hamas and Islamic Jihad – independent of one another – stated that Gaza was the place.

As with the use of the malicious software "Xtreme Rat", which infested the Israeli police's computer network, Norwegian researchers concluded that "the attackers used dynamic DNS [Domain Name System] providers to periodically shift the Internet addresses of their control networks, but that those addresses nearly always traced back to networks in Gaza assigned to a hosting provider in Ramallah in the West Bank".[45]

Thus, to sum up, we see that both Hamas and Islamic Jihad not only support the electronic jihad, but that both political movements have incorporated hackers and technological units in their armed brigades. This support is based on the notion that every part of the resistance is important and desirable as long as it hurts the occupation. Nevertheless, we have seen that their use of the technology does not necessarily mean that it must be used for offensive purposes. Rather, it is just as much used to support soldiers on the battlefield by encrypting infrastructure and jamming the Israelis' means of communication.

Although we do not have a clear explanation of why these units emerged when they did, as the different factors most likely overlap, we do know from the interviewees that it was partly done to keep pace with the technological development of the Israelis. Furthermore, the development and implementation of electronic units in Hamas and Islamic Jihad has been done with the help of state support from other Arab nations.

8

DOES MATTER REALLY MATTER?
PALESTINIAN AMBIVALENCE
ABOUT ELECTRONIC JIHAD

Palestinian hacktivism is part of a bigger coalition of groups, strategies and goals that constitute the Palestinian resistance. So far, as I have elaborated on the different parts of the Palestinian hacker environment, it could seem as if there is absolute support for the phenomenon, as if hacktivism, or electronic jihad, was not only positive in itself but also a viable means for change.

However, I should note that, although hacktivism has had some kind of breakthrough in the Palestinian political sphere, that is not to say that it has penetrated every aspect of society. On the contrary, there are several parties that have not taken a clear stance on the issue because they have not needed to (it has simply not been relevant to them). Furthermore, as my interviews with a militant from the al-Aqsa Martyrs' Brigade and a politician for PFLP sitting on the Palestinian Legislative Council (PLC) (both anonymized) show, they are not necessarily limited to being indifferent to Palestinian hacktivism but are somewhat opposed to it. That is not to say that the militants and the politicians of PFLP are representative of their armed faction or their party. Rather, this chapter shows that they do represent some views held by Palestinians that should be presented in order not to illustrate Palestinian hacktivism as being supported by every Palestinian. On the contrary, there are some Palestinians who deem it a threat to the image of the Palestinian resistance.

HACKTIVISM AND THE SECULAR RESISTANCE: "IT IS ONLY A MORALE BOOST"

Sitting in an office in one of West Bank's many refugee camps, I met a fighter from the al-Aqsa Martyrs' Brigade, a Palestinian man released in 2010 from an Israeli prison after serving six years for "making bombs, but mostly being a member of the brigade".[1]

During the interview – in a period of failed negotiations between the Palestinian Authorities and Israel – the militant stressed the importance of the resistance appearing civilized and conducting itself "the right way". Thus, how the media portrayed them was one of the most important challenges for the resistance today as, according to him, they had learned from the experiences of the 1970s and 1980s. As he elaborated on his view of hacktivism, it was quite clear that the Palestinian hacktivist attacks did not fit with his picture of correctly conducted resistance. He stated that:

> With all due respect, the hackers try to hack Israeli websites
> just as international organizations try to hack the websites of

respected peaceful countries. I am not supporting this method. Or, rather… We do not support this way because it brings a bad reputation to our resistance. We want a peaceful culture.[2]

This was followed up with the idea that the hackers made "the Americans and the rest of the world get the opinion that we are all terrorists".[3] Furthermore, even if the hackers' activities fitted within the narrative of peaceful resistance, he stated that it had no importance other than a morale boost for the Palestinian people, since it had no power to actually change Israeli political decisions on the ground:

> If the Israeli media writes about the hacking, what was written [on the defaced website] and what happened, it is nevertheless only a morale boost. So, they will not find any real information that will strengthen the resistance or which it will benefit from.[4]

Although he linked the electronic resistance to the need to gather information from within Israel, he stated that they preferred using other sources as informants. Additionally, he implied that they had been wiretapping the Israeli Knesset and got advance information about a military operation in the village of Ayn Arik, outside Ramallah, during the Second Intifada. However, I should note, his claim is highly improbable, especially in regard to the known capabilities of the al-Aqsa Martyrs' Brigade.

Although he stated that he and the brigade had not rejected armed struggle, he more than once stressed the importance of the political decisions within the party (Fatah), but considered that the most important tool of resistance at the time was the boycott of Israeli products. He compared the hackers with the international BDS (Boycott, Sanctions and Divestments) movement: "We thank the West, the foreigners that boycott Israeli products which is a better means than that of the hackers."[5]

The PFLP and PLC member I interviewed shared the views of the al-Aqsa militant. She dismissed negotiation as a tool of liberation, but stated that the resistance was multifaceted and consisted of different means. Like the member of the al-Aqsa Martyrs' Brigade, while not being against it, she dismissed hacktivism as a major part of the resistance. She made a clear separation between the physical and digital sphere:

> First of all, the digital world is digital and it is important that we know that. Secondly, there is a technological development in the world and thus, the supporters of the Palestinian people develop tools to show the world what the occupation is doing. [...] It is a new phenomenon but it cannot replace the situation on the ground.[6]

This separation proved to be crucial in her way of analyzing the needs and impact of the electronic resistance and hacktivist teams, not just for the resistance in general, but the gains that, in theory, could be achieved by its use.

It is important to note that she was far more positive towards the phenomenon than the militant of the al-Aqsa Martyrs'

Brigade. When asked whether she thought hacktivism a good tool, she answered positively. However, as the above quotation shows, it was not an issue of positive or negative features, but rather one of prioritization. Whereas the struggle on the ground – described by her as "real" – was the preferred tool to obtain change, the electronic resistance was limited to being "an approach" among several.

As the electronic resistance by virtue was digital, it could not reflect what was happening on the ground, and thus it could not be real – as opposed to demonstrations, boycotts and armed struggle, to mention a few. Since the occupation manifested itself as a physical presence through checkpoints, walls and occupying forces, the resistance also necessarily had to manifest itself through physicality.

This was shared by the militant of the al-Aqsa Brigade, who questioned the "real gains" of electronic resistance:

> The digital world will never bring us anything on the ground, and now I have to go on the Internet and hack the website of the Hebrew Channel 2 where it says that the al-Aqsa Brigade welcomes you. Of course, it does not benefit us on the ground. We want action on the ground and something that forces the Israelis from our land.[7]

Although the PFLP member thought the hackers' attack on Israeli computers was a good thing, she dismissed the notion that hacking the Israeli cyber-infrastructure led to great losses for the occupation, stating: "Well, it is a way to annoy the occupation."[8]

This aspect of materiality is something that will be discussed further when the ideological dispute between the secular and Islamist parties is assessed later on in this chapter. For now it is worth noting that the part of the secular resistance that was interviewed, albeit with internal differences in their approach to the phenomenon, was dismissive regarding hacktivism. It was considered either unimportant in comparison to the already existing resistance on the ground (PFLP) or as a potential threat to the image of the Palestinians' struggle as a legitimate resistance (the al-Aqsa Martyrs' Brigade).

So apparently, though not new, the Islamist parties such as Hamas and Islamic Jihad not only support the electronic resistance but have in addition integrated electronic brigades into their military units – the Izz al-Din al-Qassam Brigade and the al-Quds Brigade. Furthermore, there are several hacktivist teams such as Gaza Hacker Team. On the other hand, the secular parties such as PFLP and Fatah/ the al-Aqsa Martyrs' Brigade are against it or deem it unimportant for the struggle. It could be perceived as a dichotomy between the secular and religious parties; yet it is a fundamental contradiction in the Palestinian resistance going back to the late 1980s with the emergence of Hamas and the Oslo Agreement. In addition, it is a question of "reality" and the perception of materiality.

THE ASPECT OF MATERIALITY: SECULARISM VERSUS RELIGION

As the issue of materiality – i.e. the dichotomy between the virtual and physical realm – was apparent, not only within the secular groups, but also to a certain degree within Hamas, it is necessary to stress that this is not a particularly new discussion. The main question is: can only material property that can be touched or seen be considered "real"? How do we for example describe what a megabyte actually looks or feels like; it certainly is immaterial, yet simultaneously is considered to be real? To understand this issue, it is necessary to explain materiality and how the necessity of physicality is entrenched in our way of thinking – as it is a way of organizing daily life and how we perceive and interpret it. Through the centuries scholars have described the physical organization of production, and how the introduction of new means of production (changes in the societal basis) not only changes the method of production but also, for example, the dynamics and power relations of the workplace.

If one looks up the noun "Object" in the Cambridge Dictionary, one finds a rather narrow definition of the term as something strictly tangible: "A thing that you can see or touch but that is not usually a living animal, plant, or person: a solid/material/physical object."[9] However, on the issue of materiality, the discussion is more complex.

One example is Paul Leonardi who, by assessing virtual materiality, suggests that the physical matter of objects does not necessarily define materiality itself, but rather its performativity. Examples provided are scholars who do not use the noun "materiality" but rather the adjective "material", describing intangible objects such as "software". Wanda Orlikowski, for example, uses "material" to describe groupware software, when the technology embodies particular symbolic and material properties. Furthermore, and more importantly, all of this software Leonardi refers to – described as "material" – has technological properties that are able to perform an action (financial transactions, virtual phone calls, reading a newspaper). Thus he states that: "In other words, calling something material emphasizes its performativity – the notion that it provides people with capabilities that they can use to accomplish their goals."[10]

Materiality is thus not necessarily a dichotomy between the tangible and intangible, but rather something that is possible to transcend depending on the object's use. This performativity of an object is at the same time not something limited to the immaterial such as software (try to touch an email if you can) but can be explained through what Marx described as the necessity of use value. The matter of a table or a hammer is of no importance before it is used within the context of human action. This notion is shared by Leonardi, and thus he states, on the issue of digital materiality:

> This discussion of affordances pushes us to ask whether physical matter really matters at all. If what is important about "material" artifacts is how they are perceived and subsequently used, as opposed to what they are made of, then using the adjective "material" to denote that an object has a physical substance would seem relatively unimportant for explaining the contours of social interaction. … Thus, when those researchers describe digital artifacts as having "material" properties, aspects, or features, we might safely say that what makes them "material" is that they provide capabilities that afford or constrain action.[11]

This is something which can be written about at great length, but the point is to highlight that the notion of materiality depends on whether materiality is interpreted according to the narrow or the broad definition of the term – which lets us explain the conflicting views of the PFLP and the Islamist parties on electronic resistance and hacktivism.

Since the Israelis control the Palestinian population through a variety of tools, such as military checkpoints, walls, military camps, soldiers on the ground throughout the whole West Bank and a physical blockade of the Gaza Strip, the occupation does to a large degree manifest itself as a physical construct. As the dialectical relationship between the manifestation of the occupation and the resistance to it has developed and interacted, historically the resistance has been largely physical: sabotage, labor strikes, demonstrations and military campaigns. Some of them have targeted the occupation in general while others have been short-term and tactical – such as the Friday demonstrations which are often limited to the issue of the wall.

This seems to have formed the PFLP's notion of 'real' resistance. Hacktivism, Internet activism and the use of the digital realm, while not essentially bad, are disconnected from the real world. As the PFLP representative stated, "the digital world is digital and it is important that we know that", and "The electronic resistance enters the part of the world which is digital and through the computer, not the reality".[12] Thus she makes a clear distinction between the materiality of the "real world" and the "immateriality" of the digital world. As the occupation is embodied in physical obstacles and actions, the resistance has to be expressed in the same manner.

On the other hand, the Islamist parties consider electronic resistance useful, with its possibility to penetrate the Israeli cyber-infrastructure. Consequently, its use to hack bank accounts, take down Israeli websites, prevent wiretapping/espionage and spread the Palestinian issue to the rest of the world transcends the border between the tangible and intangible and henceforth becomes "material'" where no materiality exists as such.

Also, on the point of virtuality, materiality and what is rendered real: it seems as if hackers, in the PFLP member's perception of them, cannot be rendered as active subjects, but are rather isolated objects confined within a geographical border, in this case the boy's room or the house – i.e. not on the streets. The physical obstacle of the house's walls is something which the hacker is not able to transcend in order to influence the physical world where the "real" struggle is being fought. Thus, the hacker is deemed a singular and isolated object; a completely isolated individual and only subject to their own laws. The hackers possess no material or spatial character and are never able to transcend the border between the digital and physical realms.

HOW TO RESIST, THAT IS THE QUESTION

The issue of supporting hacktivism and the electronic resistance is, however, not limited to the importance of the digital realm. It is also something that has to be contextualized within a period of time within which the different groups in the Palestinian resistance are operating.

As noted earlier, on the development and digitalization of the Palestinian resistance, it is facing a watershed in a period of broken negotiations, a highly unpopular security cooperation between the Palestinian Authority and Israel, and international diplomacy to get Palestine recognized as a state, to mention a few. This has of course created a split between the political parties and groups that support non-violent resistance and negotiations, and those that do not recognize Israel and uphold confrontation and armed resistance as a tool to liberate the homeland.

This was particularly striking when the member of the al-Aqsa Martyrs' Brigade referred to the "political decisions" within the movement – no fewer than fourteen times. As the brigade is the armed wing of Fatah this must be seen in the context of a period when negotiations as a tactic are not dismissed, with Mahmoud Abbas proclaiming that there will be no intifada as long as he is the leader, and the al-Aqsa Martyrs' Brigade having put down their weapons in the West Bank.[13] If the situation should change with a spontaneous uprising, a new Palestinian leadership in the West Bank or the success of the unification process between Hamas and Fatah, the notion of electronic resistance could be altered: "The apartheid wall or the military checkpoints which are there now, it will never stop anyone of the fighters to attack. It will never stop us. The only thing is a Palestinian political decision."[14]

This was confirmed when the militant said everyone had to bow to the political decisions (within the movement) and stated at the end of the interview: "If we get a political decision to fight electronically we will do it – if they consider the electronic war or the electronic jihad."[15] Thus, it is clear that the objections to hacking are not necessarily ideological, but rather a tactical notion within the framework of the present situation of Fatah and its armed wing. For Hamas, Islamic Jihad and other groupings which from the beginning of the Oslo Accords dismissed them and the negotiations as a means to achieve liberation, the situation is diametrically different.

However, the dividing line is not merely ideological, but also geographical. For instance, the al-Aqsa Martyrs' Brigade is not unified across geographical borders, for example between the West Bank and the Gaza Strip. The armed wing of Fatah in the Gaza Strip has persisted with armed operations against Israel at the same time as its West Bank counterpart has been pacified – the latest example being during the escalations in the summer of 2014. The documentary "At the Heart of the Siege: Hacker Force" tried to show the variety of hacker groups in the Gaza Strip. It included an interview with a hacker, Abu Yasser, from the al-Aqsa Martyrs' Brigade:

> We have a special team that follows up with Israeli affairs
> including the electronic resistance unit. This team attempts
> to hack Israeli websites, gathers information about the enemy,
> tries to weaken the Zionists' morale, and sends the messages.
> The group also attacks websites and changes them, like
> changing the homepage, putting a logo of Palestine or a photo
> of a baby girl killed by the Israeli army and then saying "We
> are coming to you".[16]

In other words, the view of the militant does not necessarily constitute the view of the brigade as a whole, but rather portrays its situation in the West Bank. The al-Aqsa Martyrs' Brigade is not, and has never been a united front. Thus, the ideological line on hacktivism that splits the al-Aqsa Martyrs' Brigade in the West Bank and its counterparts in the Gaza Strip is a line going back to the Oslo Accords and their legality.

Thus, the differing views on the effect and usefulness of hacktivism are not caused by politico-religious divisions, but rather depend on attitudes for or against resistance at large. It is precisely this division that has made different Palestinian parties grow and shrink. For example, while Hamas had existed for several decades without any significant growth, with the beginning of the Oslo agreement and the PLO leaving the resistance the movement was able to fill the void that was left. On the other hand, the political party Ḥizb al-Taḥrīr al-Islāmī (the Islamic Party of Liberation) has the same goal of establishing an Islamic society, but strictly through the practice of daʿwa (proselytizing), and has consequently failed to gain a significant following.[17]

We will see that the diverging notions on hacktivism is not an issue of being Palestinian Islamist or secular when I assess the views of the popular resistance organization, Stop the Wall Campaign – a campaign largely composed of members from the secular Ḥizb al-Shaʿb (The People's Party), the former Palestinian communist party. This assessment is done for two reasons: first, to present the views of some parts of the Palestinian popular resistance; second, to show that secular Palestinian organizations do, in fact, also support Palestinian hacktivism.

HACKTIVISM AND THE POPULAR RESISTANCE

As the Stop the Wall Campaign is one of the largest or at least most active popular organizations working on the ground against the

Israeli occupation – and represented throughout the West Bank by different committees – I conducted an interview with its main coordinator Jamāl Jumaʿ to get an understanding of how they viewed the electronic resistance. It was clearly different from the PFLP and the al-Aqsa Martyrs' Brigade/Fatah.

For Jumaʿ and the Stop the Wall Campaign, the popular resistance – consisting of all popular factions such as trade unions, political parties, universities and grassroots organizations – was the most effective tool to end the occupation.

It should seem that, within this narrative of resistance, the hackers would not fit in as they perceive themselves to be a part of the armed resistance. However, Jumaʿ supported their actions, but by applying a different framework:

> I consider this as a part of the popular resistance. As it is
> done by people … by civilians who are unarmed and who
> have this as their field of specialty. So they do their job from
> their point of view from where they are staying, from how
> they understand how to do it. So this is a part of the popular
> resistance, part of harming the occupation.[18]

He held the same opinion as the parties that can be considered pro-resistance, stating that hacktivism complemented the rest of the resistance, as hacking constituted a smaller part within a larger whole – such as the BDS movement. Nevertheless, this view was based on a narrow definition of what the armed resistance entailed: primarily taking up arms against Israeli soldiers, as the computer, according to Jumaʿ, could not by itself be used as a weapon. Since the hackers have most likely never touched a weapon, they are considered civilians engaging in the popular struggle within the modern context of digitalization. This is in addition to the fact that the hacktivist never harmed anyone physically.

Hacktivism is not necessarily limited to being a tool to harm the occupation – for example economically – but also in order to spread information and mobilize the international community. For Jumaʿ, hacking was an essential tool to gain attention from the rest of the world, while the operations showed that the Palestinians were not a backward people without any experience with modern technology:

> It is widely grabbing their [the Western world's] attention
> and it is also showing that the Palestinians are not primitive.
> So they are very well educated, they are up to date with the
> international development, the worldwide development, the
> electronic development so they have a very smart talent:
> People who are doing such an amazing, effective work.[19]

Thus, he stated, hacktivism "is an advantage and adds value to the Palestinian resistance or the Palestinian people's history of resistance".[20]

When we discussed the history of hacktivism and its earlier encounters, where popular movements have cooperated with hackers (as in Seattle in 1999 during the protests against the World Trade Organization when the Electrohippies attempted to slow down the WTO conference networks at the same time as protesters gathered in the streets outside), he nevertheless held that the political and organizational independence of the hackers was important. The magic of the hack was its spontaneity and its ability to penetrate the Israeli cyber-infrastructure from the hackers' own point of view. As a force it should not be limited by political parties or organizations.

Furthermore, on the support of hacktivism in the traditional resistance and the dispute between the Islamist and secular parties, he expressed frustration with the latter group:

> You know, I think this has something to do with the ways the parties are managing themselves and how they are alerted, how much they are alerted to the occupation. It seems like the situation within Fatah and the secular parties are much more relaxed than the parties who are under attack – under serious attack.[21]

However, Juma' noted that the use of electronic means such as hacking was not only an ideological dispute between the secular and Islamist parties, but also a result of the diametrically different situations in which they lived. As the Islamist parties Hamas and Islamic Jihad were under much more pressure than, for example, Fatah, they had to find different means of resistance that would not endanger their operations.

PART III

WHEN THE GUNS FALL SILENT

9

A CONTINUATION OF
THE ARMED STRUGGLE?

I have written about Gaza Hacker Team, Islamic Jihad and Hamas, what they do, what means they are employing, and why we still need a more elaborate discussion on the nature of Palestinian hacktivism. That is, whether Gaza Hacker Team is correct in stating that hacktivism is a continuation of the armed struggle. In order not to fallaciously label electronic jihad as cyberterrorism, cyber-vandalism or cyber-crime, or create a meaningless dichotomization between hacktivism and patriotic hacking as done by Michael Dahan[1] (elaborated upon later in this chapter), we need to discuss what part of the Palestinian resistance it constitutes.

For example, is Gaza Hacker Team a continuation of the armed struggle, as they proclaim? And is then the political nature of the means and acts, and the framework that Gaza Hacker Team operates within, qualitatively the same as is the case with Hamas and Islamic Jihad?

In part one of this book, the development, the changing rhetoric and discourse, and the means employed were discussed in order to establish the development and context of Palestinian electronic jihad: from initially wanting to defeat Israel militarily and simultaneously counter the symbolic violence produced in the conflict in the beginning, via the First and Second Intifadas, to the situation today.

Yet, as the PFLP and other Palestinian groups hijacked airplanes to simply show that there was such a thing as the Palestinians, the necessity of getting the world's attention is still evident today. And why should it not be? The main problem, illustrated by the example of non-violent resistance, is that of a theater performance: "Non-violence", Arundhati Roy states, "is a piece of theatre. You need an audience. What can you do when you have no audience?"[2]

Thus, the necessity of acting to make the world comprehend the situation on the ground in Palestine has not been limited to hijacking airplanes. For example, one of the main goals of the Palestinian grassroots movements is to make the world aware of the Palestinians' situation under the occupation. The same applies to demonstrations, general strikes, participating in international solidarity organizations, writing articles and narratives, creating blogs and even conducting stone-throwing – albeit the intent is not always expressed explicitly.

The necessity of giving the international community a message, or rather an appeal, is thus something that transcends the physical/digital borderline between demonstrations and direct action in the physical realm and Palestinian hacktivism in the digital realm. Let me elaborate by first using the Palestinian hacktivist group KDMS Team as an example, and then, later on, moving to Gaza Hacker Team.

RAISING THE WORLD'S AWARENESS: KDMS TEAM

Although Gaza Hacker Team has been one of the most active and best known Palestinian hacktivist teams, there have nevertheless been several other Palestinian teams that have made the headlines – not only in Palestine and in Israel but also globally. Some of them have been active for a shorter period of time and then died away – a rather typical feature of many hacktivist teams, often continuing their work under a different name or aligning themselves with a different team.

As the Palestinian KDMS Team made headlines through-out the world in 2013, their targets were qualitatively different to those of Gaza Hacker Team. Whereas the majority of Gaza Hacker Team's penetrations were directed towards the Israeli cyber-infrastructure, every single website defaced by KDMS Team was foreign. That is probably one of the reasons the team got so much attention in the first place – with *International Business Times* and *Spiegel Online* covering the campaign.[3]

In addition, no irrelevant websites were being defaced, but rather the websites of big companies such as WhatsApp (the cross-platform messaging service owned by Facebook), Alexa (subsidiary of Amazon providing commercial web traffic data), Avira, BitDefender and AVG (all of the latter being antivirus software companies) to mention a few – all within the period of 8 to 12 October 2013.

However, their activities did not last for long and the group officially ceased to exist after April 2014; at least in terms of significant activity. A main reason for their declining activity might be the American grey hat hacker th3 j35t3r (The Jester),[4] also known by his real name Mark Walker. He is an American hacktivist who targets websites and groups, often, but not limited to, Islamists – according to him, driven by "American patriotism". His targets included the KDMS Team, which, after targeting the international websites, was doxed[5] by th3 j35t3r. He published the identities and names of potential members of the team, many of them residing in Gaza, on Pastebin, a web application where anyone can store plain text – a popular tool of hackers disclaiming information.

There is no reason to take this information at face value as his method is questionable, in this case comparing Twitter activity, and as previous doxings have additionally proved to have identified persons who have never had any affiliation with the targeted groups.

As I had made contact with Gaza Hacker Team, being able to get their own account of their operations, ideology and organizational structure, I tried to do the same with KDMS Team. Through our correspondence, they did confirm that every single member of the team was Palestinian.[6] According to them, it was not because of th3 j35t3r's doxing attempt that they went underground, but because they "have been working in secret for personal interests".[7] Also, more importantly, they stated that "We have been hacking for a long time under different names".[8]

In addition, they had, like Gaza Hacker Team, no affiliations to any political party, and had made no political statements in the form of a declaration. However, they differed in one important respect. Whereas Gaza Hacker Team felt that they had no support from any political faction, KDMS Team answered that: "All of the Palestinian people support the resistance in all of its shapes."[9] Also, the electronic resistance was to a large degree a part of the traditional resistance – i.e. every Palestinian resisted in the way he/she was able , whether in the digital or physical realm. Thus, KDMS Team and Gaza Hacker Team diverged on their ideas of hacktivist campaigns as armed or popular struggle.

As Gaza Hacker Team and KDMS Team were divided on the issue of struggling against the occupation not by their goals, but by their tactics, namely the geographical locations of their hacked websites, the political content of their defacements were similar. While Gaza Hacker Team highlighted political causes such as the Palestinian prisoners on hunger strike or the latest attacks on the Gaza Strip, KDMS Team focused on the Palestinian cause in its entirety. As they noted briefly, "We attack global sites and not local sites".[10] Yet, since many of the defacements by Gaza Hacker Team could be perceived as threatening, the KDMS Team's goal was to spread awareness of what was going on to the rest of the world.

Thus, we might compare the hijacking of airplanes (as the campaigns made the world aware that a Palestinian people did exist), or Arundhati Roy's comparison of non-violence and theater to KDMS Team's campaigns against the different websites. For example, what they wrote on the defaced website of Bitdefender is illustrative for the Palestinian campaigns of raising awareness about the Palestinian cause:

> There is a land called Palestine on the earth/This land has been stolen by Zionist/Do you know it?/Palestinian people has the right to live in peace/Deserve to liberate their land and release all prisoners from israeli [sic] jails/We want peace/

With maps showing the demographic development in Palestine and Israel, with ever more Palestinian land being appropriated by the Israelis, they ended their message with "Long Live Palestine" and an emoticon holding the Palestinian flag.[11] As they themselves expressed in the interview, "We hack foreign sites to deliver a message to the world".[12]

Thus, by virtue of their own statements about wanting to send a message to the world, and the content of their defacement, it seems, so far, that KDMS Team is a part of an older Palestinian tradition of countering the symbolic violence as already described. By hacking international websites and creating an international awareness of what is going on, KDMS Team attempts to spur support for the Palestinian cause.

Although I will return to the nature of KDMS Team's hacks later, we might ask how proficient and capable KDMS Team was. Obviously it was embarrassing for large anti-virus companies such as AVG, but was the defacement of the website a result of sophisticated tools and world-class hackers? Some would say not.

As the different websites under attack tried to regain control over their domains, it became increasingly clear that no customer information or sensitive data had been compromised. Rather, what KDMS Team had done was a common DNS hijacking.[13]

The DNS is briefly, though not precisely, summed up as something that converts any IP address (consisting of numbers alone, such as "192.0.43.10") to the web address that you see in your browser, for example "www.google.com". In other words, KDMS Team had not been able to gain access to the database of AVG itself, but rather rerouted the AVG traffic to another website where the message was shown.

There are two ways this can be done: First, KDMS Team could simply have guessed the passwords of the different websites and logged in as administrators. However, this is highly unlikely. Secondly, they might have tricked the Network Solution – where the DNS records are managed – into changing the passwords of the website. Thus, one can discuss how complicated the KDMS Team hacks really were and how educated the members are; but, on the other hand, if it gets the job done, why do it the hard way?

TRANSLATING THE PRINCIPLES OF DIRECT ACTION TO THE VIRTUAL REALM: GAZA HACKER TEAM

On 16 October 2012 a group of Palestinian activists sat down and blocked route 443, the route between Tel Aviv and Jerusalem. For thirty minutes the group managed to block the route until Israeli police officers removed them.

The campaign is valuable in two senses: First of all, by sitting down in the middle of the road, the activists effectively managed to block the access of drivers and passengers to a public, physical realm, mainly Tel Aviv, Jerusalem and any other stop on the way. Thus, there are without doubt similarities to DDoS attacks in the digital sphere, as I have outlined previously, since both DDoS and the sit-in demonstration hinder access to a particular physical or digital site. Whether it is your online bank account which you cannot access because the website of the bank has been brought down by hackers, or you are unable to access the bank in its physical manifestation because you simply cannot reach it when the road has been blocked, these are in their essence qualitatively identical actions.

Secondly, when the demonstrators were arrested after blocking route 443, one of the organizers stated that as long as the Palestinians were suffering under occupation, Israeli daily life would not continue as usual.[14] Seemingly, mimicking the violence that Palestinians are being subjected to and breaking the normality of Israeli daily lives are features in the Palestinian resistance not limited to one particular set of means such as suicide bombings or hacktivists defacing a website in general, or a personal account in particular, Nor is mimicking violence limited to blocking an Israelis road by direct action in the physical realm.

If one chooses to assess Palestinian resistance as being various means employed against the Israeli occupation, determined by specific historical conditions, then we see that hacktivism a priori fits within its narrative, history and semantics. That is to say, Palestinian hacktivism is a means to challenge the occupation and occupier in the digital sphere, either by raising the awareness of the international community or by breaching the normality of Israeli daily lives.

Even when it comes to the goal of imposing economic pressure on the occupier (Gaza Hacker Team's program of principles), we see similarities to Palestinian grassroots action. For example, the demonstrators participating in the Friday demonstrations have expressed the aim of raising the costs of the occupation to a level which would be intolerable.[15]

Thus, Palestinian hacktivism works to disrupt and interfere with the occupation with the goal of ending the situation on the ground in occupied Palestine. Furthermore, as mentioned, defacements of websites can be compared to political graffiti, and it is relevant as the latter has been documented as entailing intervention in the established power relations between the occupier and the occupied.[16] The similarities are not limited to the visual modifications of the wall or the website, but also insofar as the hacktivists are in fact deliberately intruding into foreign and alien spaces just as graffiti artists and taggers do in the physical realm.

For example, Gaza Hacker Team's campaigns epitomize exactly the kind of popular resistance that Darweish and Rigby term "polemical resistance": "[w]e oppose the occupier by voicing protest and trying to encourage others of the need to maintain the struggle" – i.e. the morale boost that the militant of the al-Aqsa Martyrs' Brigade so easily dismissed.[17]

It is precisely this distinction that Michael Dahan, from the Israeli Sapir College, seems incapable of making when he attempts to dichotomize the term *hacktivist* and what he himself brands as "patriotic hacker" – with explicit references to the Israel/Palestine conflict. By using Israel and "the Muslim world" as an example, he follows the same definition for hacktivism as applied in this book, and rightly so. Yet this definition cannot be used to describe Palestinian hackers (among others) because, "the patriotic hacker", Dahan states, "enjoys a different set of motivations than those mentioned above and tends to be closer in nature to the cyber criminal or cyber terrorist".

Furthermore, "As opposed to the hacker and the hacktivist, political ideology tends toward conservatism and nationalism".[18]

Dahan's argument is that because the term "hacktivism" was initially meant to refer to the use of technology for the advancement of human rights, so-called patriotic hacking – which, according to him, Gaza Hacker Team obviously would be a part of – must necessarily be excluded from it as hacktivism is an "advancement of political causes" while patriotic hacking is "defense of the homeland".[19]

It is hard to see how these are dichotomies and mutually exclusive as the liberation of occupied territories is certainly a political cause – and even a progressive one as it works for the implementation of human rights for those under military rule. It would be like claiming that omelets cannot be made out of eggs because eggs are a component in making a cake.

Although resisting occupation through the means of hacking has a different goal than free speech on the Internet, they are qualitatively the same. Although feminists today have different goals and are conducting different political campaigns than the suffragettes, they are still part of the same historical movement.

For example, as I have shown, Gaza Hacker Team and other Palestinian hacktivist groups such as the KDMS Team do in fact have a lot in common with the popular Palestinian struggle on the ground in terms of goals and means. It is hard to see the term "patriotic hacker" as any less delegitimizing than the term "cyber-terrorist", as Dahan himself falsely states that a patriotic hacker, "[t]ends to be closer in nature to the cyber criminal or cyber terrorist".[20] Apparently it is not what you do, but what you work for that defines who you are. Even if that work is to end the Israeli occupation.

Perhaps what Dahan fails to grasp is what Žižek outlines as the dialectics of the actually existing situation and that of its expectations (although, I should mention, Žižek used dialectics while discussing Stalinist Soviet and the utopian expectations of it[21]) – i.e. the space and the positive content that fills it. Dahan is obviously correct when he points out that groups such as Gaza Hacker Team are "further to the right" (if that is even a possible measure for the contradictory politico-religious content of Gaza Hacker Team) when we consider their slogans, rhetoric and self-representation in a political void.

Yet once again we have to return to the *content* of their phrasing, on the one hand, and the *essence* of it on the other. While they do in fact use what can be perceived as extremist language and references, they nevertheless simultaneously open up a space of utopian expectations which are the full, ensuing rights, sovereignty and dignity of the Palestinians when they are no longer occupied.

Thus, the conclusion is that the hacktivism of Gaza Hacker Team is a new tendency in the Palestinian resistance and necessarily a part of it – enabled by technological development globally, regionally and locally. The forms of hacktivism and its means that I have used as examples in this part show that there are in fact clear parallels between them and the non-violent popular struggle even though Gaza Hacker Team claims to identify itself with the armed struggle.

Whereas the Palestinian demonstrators blocked route 443, Gaza Hacker Team translates these principles of direct action into the digital sphere by blocking access to particular websites. As

Palestinian taggers intervene in the established power relations between the occupied and occupier by spraying walls, Gaza Hacker Team, KDMS Team and other Palestinian hacktivist teams translate these principles to the digital sphere by virtue of defacements. Furthermore, as these activists are employing these means in the physical sphere in order to make the rest of world aware of the Palestinians, raise the costs of the occupation or impose mimetic violence, we see that that Palestinian hacktivist teams have exactly the same goals when conducting electronic jihad.

Thus, my conclusion is that Gaza Hacker Team is incorrect in stating that their electronic jihad is a continuation of the armed struggle, and that KDMS Team is correct in identifying themselves with the popular struggle. By virtue of their actions, these two hacktivist teams translate the Palestinian principles of popular protests to the digital sphere, and not the military tactics of the Palestinian armed groups.

It might be necessary to return briefly to the analysis of Palestinian stone-throwing – that is, as not necessarily non-violent (yet, simultaneously non-armed) but as a means of direct action. As Jordan and Taylor point out, "the notion of violence in cyberspace involves complexities, if not at times absurdities, because the conception of non-violence prevalent in social movements involves an inherent physicality that is absent in cyberspace".[22]

They conclude that it is more feasible to focus on direct action and hacktivism instead of *non-violent* direct action as a whole.[23] For example, on the issue of the legality of direct action, it should be clear that the hacking of Israeli websites is illegal according to the laws existing today, yet laws can be ignored or transgressed. The modus operandi of civil disobedience, for example, is that it ignores unjust laws, and "[d]irect action is not only the behaviour of activists 'in the field' but is also the effects that are supposed to flow from these actions".[24] Then, if I may paraphrase the activist from Walajah quoted in the second chapter: the hacking of Israeli websites is not non-violent but it is a part of the popular resistance. We call it popular resistance, not peaceful resistance, so it includes hacktivism.

However, the definition of hacktivism as a form of armed struggle or not might also depend on one's point of view. For example, I have already shown how Israel's Prime Minister Benyamin Netanyahu and the Israeli government consider the cyber-threat as an issue for the Israeli military, and thus implicitly as a form of armed resistance. Yet in 1998 when the Israeli hacker Ehud Tenenbaum (the Analyzer) hacked computers belonging among others to NASA, the Pentagon, the US Air Force and the US Navy, "Israeli public figures took a much more conciliatory attitude to Tenenbaum's activities and their implications".[25] And Prime Minister Netanyahu's first comment was that the Analyzer is "damn good" (although adding that he could be "very dangerous too").[26]

So, even though Gaza Hacker Team does not constitute a continuation of the armed struggle, does that necessarily mean that there are no forms of Palestinian hacking that are a part of the militarization of the Internet and implicitly a continuation of the Palestinian armed struggle? I would argue that, in fact, there is, but in order to describe that particular phenomenon we have to turn to Hamas and Palestinian Islamic Jihad.

HAMAS, ISLAMIC JIHAD, AND THE MILITARIZATION OF THE INTERNET

Today, we have come to a situation which is diametrically opposed to that foreseen by the technology-optimists quoted in the introduction. Stuxnet, Flame and Duqu are only one small part of it and only present a fraction of its implications. While Gaza Hacker Team is not a part of the militarization of the Internet as a continuation of the Palestinian armed resistance, I will argue that, in fact, Hamas' and Palestinian Islamic Jihad's cyber-battalions are. How does that make any sense?

First of all, if we are to place Gaza Hacker Team into the category of militarization of the Internet, it must necessarily have some implications for the equivalent means employed in the public, physical realm discussed above. For example, if DDoS attacks by virtue of being DDoS attacks constitute a militarization of the Internet when employed against the Israeli government, agencies and companies, does that not necessarily imply that Palestinian sit-in demonstrations and graffiti constitute the militarization of the public, physical realm? Activists and demonstrators would deny that is so.

The same applies to leaking information, as was the case with Edward Snowden's leaks from the NSA. Of course, there is a persisting debate whether Snowden's actions were legitimate or not, but it should be needless to say that the leaks did not constitute a militarization of the public-physical realm. It was not particularly surprising that the chiefs of the national surveillance programs in the West stated that Snowden had handed the, always anonymous, "terrorists" a gift.[27]

When it comes to the militarization of the Internet, it is somewhat ironic that it is those who are a part of and responsible for its militarization that accuse Edward Snowden, demonstrators such as Occupy Wall Street and the rest of the usual suspects of being the helpers of terrorists (at best). It is for example first and foremost military officials who increasingly think of the Internet as another platform of warfare,[28] as when the Israeli Major General Aviv Kovachi stated that "cyber, in my modest opinion, will soon be revealed to be the biggest revolution in warfare, more than gunpowder and the utilization of air power in the last century".[29]

One of the features of the militarization is for example the increasing surveillance of pretty much everyone. The logic of today is not that you are innocent until the opposite has been proven, but, in fact, that everyone is guilty until the opposite has been proven. Ronald J. Deibert, professor at University of Toronto, describes the "militarization" of the Internet as an "offensive information warfare" with the development of "cyber-war tools". The example used is the United States' military with its "computer hackers, ... advanced Trojan horses, viruses, and worms, and [the US] has used techniques of cyber-propaganda leading up to the conflict in Iraq".[30]

Although Deibert wrote his analysis of the Internet militarization in 2003, we see that it still has relevance today. Regarding the worms and malicious software employed by state agencies, we encountered the examples of the Israeli-American Stuxnet, Duqu and Flame earlier in this book.

The computer hackers that Deibert uses as an example have been known about for a while now, and the Israeli government announced in June 2015 that it would create a "cyber-branch" within the Israeli army to unite all of its cyber-capabilities. It would encompass defensive and offensive cyberwarfare, and intelligence collection.[31]

There are also cases where the borderline between the physical and digital spheres is fading, as is the case with the one-megaton bombs that Israel allegedly (and with emphasis on *allegedly*) possesses, with EMP (electromagnetic pulse) strike capability. Halper uses Iran as an example, illustrating how the bomb detonated 400 kilometers over the country would, coupled with cyberattacks, take out the electric power grid, communications, oil refineries and transportation, with the result of food supplies running out and the economy crashing.[32] That would obviously be a worst-case scenario, but with the overall emphasis on the threat of cyberterrorism, there should evidently be some additional worry about potential state cyberterrorism.

The use of cyber-propaganda does also constitute a part of the militarization of the Internet – which, I should note, is used by both sides in the Israeli–Palestinian conflict. Dara Kerr at CNET, for example, uses the term "weaponization" of social media, referring to the efforts by both parties to convey their messages on the Internet.[33]

The Israeli army is overly active on social media such as Facebook, Twitter and YouTube, posting updates and videos of liquidating, maiming and injuring Palestinians they deem as a "threat". Kerr, for example, documents how, after the assassination of Hamas' military leader Aḥmad Jaʿbarī in 2012, the Israeli army uploaded a "brief, silent, black-and-white" video of the airstrike on YouTube with the caption "Ahmed Jabari: Eliminated".

It is a textbook example of documenting real people being shredded to pieces with the sanitizing overtones of the wargame Call of Duty. The Izz al-Din al-Qassam Brigade sent their own message back on Twitter stating "Our blessed hands will reach your leaders wherever you are (You Opened Hell Gates on Yourselves)".[34]

The social media war is not limited to the escalation in 2012. In 2013, the Israeli newspaper *Haaretz* documented how the Israeli Prime Minister's Office recruited students who would post the "Israeli version" on social media. Although they would not identify themselves as government officials, they would be a part of the Prime Minister's Office public diplomacy arm.[35] It is what the Israelis call *hasbara*, the Hebrew word for "explanation" – though admittedly "propaganda" would be more suitable.

And it is here that we come to Hamas' and Palestinian Islamic Jihad's cyber-units, that respectively find themselves in the Izz al-Din al-Qassam Brigades and the al-Quds Brigade. Yes, Gaza Hacker Team does employ some of the same means as Hamas and Islamic Jihad, and the way the main representative of Islamic Jihad presented the use of the technology, that is, mainly defensive, it would at the outset seem opposite to the case of Gaza Hacker Team. Yet we should note Deibert's use of the term "militarization", as he considers the strictly *military* use of the technology.[36]

To elaborate, it is all about the framework in which you conduct your actions, and in the case of Hamas and Islamic Jihad their cyber-units are operating strictly within a framework of armed brigades. They do not hack for the sake of the hack itself or for the fame they could obtain, but as an extension and supplement to a modern battlefield in which electronics are becoming an inherent part of it. In other words, the electronic units of Hamas and Islamic Jihad cannot be rendered as an isolated part outside of their armed brigades, and thus constitute a continuation – or rather a modernization – of the Palestinian armed struggle. They do so by easing the work of the Palestinian soldiers by providing information, encrypting their own cyber-infrastructure and jamming communication lines, to mention a few. This is qualitatively different from the activities of, for example, Gaza Hacker Team and KDMS Team.

Gaza Hacker Team and its members are activists in the traditional sense of the term – although conducting their campaigns in the digital sphere – while the hackers of, for example, Islamic Jihad are part of a continuous and interconnected battlefield in development. What the hackers of Gaza Hacker Team do is done in their spare time, as part of a young activist collective, and in order to contribute in the way that they know how.

The mere word "hacktivism", as stated, is the blending of "activism" and "hacking" and Islamic Jihad and Hamas can thus be excluded from this definition through the narrow interpretation of the word. Hacktivism by itself, conducted by traditional activists, cannot be rendered as militarization but as a parallel development of protests in the digital era.

10

FINAL THOUGHTS

As a relatively new phenomenon, I do not dare to say what impact Palestinian hacktivism and electronic jihad will have on the Palestinian struggle against the Israeli occupation in the long term. I have 1972 in the back of my mind, when Richard Nixon arrived in China and was welcomed by the Chinese Prime Minister Zhou Enlai. Allegedly, as Nixon asked his host about the French Revolution's historical impact, Enlai responded, "That's too early to say".

Yet we should dwell somewhat on the implications of Palestinian hacktivism, to outline some of the features that have not been touched upon until now. The clues I am hinting at are the internationalization of the Palestinian struggle and the transgression of borders. Furthermore, is the way that Palestinian hacktivism is shaped necessarily and exclusively positive?

HACKTIVISM AS A CURSOR OF IDENTITY

While the different hacktivist groups such as Gaza Hacker Team are attempting to play their part in the digital sphere against the occupation, they simultaneously recreate, brand and necessarily promote themselves through the use of avatars and slogans – cloaked behind a wall of anonymity. For example, as Gaza Hacker Team and other hackers recreate themselves using catchy names with a sense of bravado (the forum participants freedom_fighter4pal and malik maṣīrihi/King of Fate come to mind), hacktivism and individualized political action is just as much a pointer of personal identity as it is for qualitative change.

That is, within this sphere of anonymity and use of avatars, there is simultaneously the construction of a macho-ideal where the "youngsters" become digital warriors, the incarnation of Ibn Khattab, and men posing with weapons – it is a continuation of a virtual *self* as a means of self-realization and subsequently a self-promotion. Furthermore, parallel to the construction of the macho-ideal, there does not seem to be any intent of working alongside the rest of Palestinian civil society in an alliance against the occupation. Thus, the hacktivist manifestation of Gaza Hacker Team becomes additionally a closed sphere reserved for its members.

On the opposite side of the field, social movements consist of anonymous masses that are doing the dirty work for the common cause. Of course, I do not intend to fetishize the social movement as if it were some kind of romanticized revolutionary vanguard, but rather to hint that some of the "old" features in the way of organizing politically have advantages that seem to have been lost.

The objections given above do, evidently, contain some shades of grey. I am not naïve in regard of the necessity of anonymity when it comes to the actions conducted by Gaza Hacker Team, or any other Palestinian hacker teams for that matter. The anonymity is undoubtedly necessary in the game of cat and mouse of the resistance and the Israeli occupation.

Furthermore, if we go past the macho-ideal as a symptom of male youngsters who will eventually grow up, we should ask ourselves if their self-representation can be analyzed through the Lacanian notion of *Objet petit a* – the object cause of desire. For example, can the way young Palestinian hackers portray themselves be seen in a Gaza-Palestinian context where there are few possibilities to find work or at least a sustainable income? The implication of that is, of course, that it will be even more difficult to get married. These factors that affect feelings of masculinity, self-worth and autonomy come in addition to the horrible living conditions in Gaza.

Then, we might analyze the macho-ideal and the Palestinian hackers' recreation of themselves into cyber-warriors as an underlying symptom, where the object of desire is the "loophole" of the digital sphere where they (for a short period of time) can be actually autonomous subjects where the rules of the occupation no longer apply. They are no longer victims of occupation; rather, in cyberspace, they become jihadism's answer to Che Guevara: Ibn Khattab.

Some might also object that it is in the nature of hacktivism to act within the framework of clandestine groups or non-hierarchical movements such as Anonymous, where whoever wants to can, and will, become an Anon; they might object on the grounds that it operates outside the boundaries of the Palestinian political parties, and is open for everyone. And, I should admit, this is obviously one of its democratic features. Yet to conduct electronic jihad requires a technical know-how beyond restarting your computer to fix a problem. Being a hacktivist, then, becomes (once again) a foreign space limited to the more highly educated section of the Palestinian population.

On the other hand, qualitatively different problems require qualitatively different solutions. There is no doubt that hacktivism, including its Palestinian equivalent, is the result of the Internet creating a new possibility-space of action simply because it is now technologically possible. With the development of the new means of production and a whole new cyber-infrastructure, commerce, dialogue and entertainment, for example, have now changed. Does hacktivism mean that we have to throw the old ways of organizing ourselves politically, or at least parts of it, into the dustbin of history?

We necessarily have to find out how these lines can be transcended as there is historical precedent for cooperation along the hacktivist–social movement line. One example, from which we can learn, is the protests against the World Trade Organization in Seattle in 1999, when hackers and the anti-globalization movement allied themselves: as both parties aimed at disrupting the WTO conference, the demonstrators and activists in the physical sphere arranged mass demonstrations and acts of civil disobedience in order to block the streets and to show their dissent.

Simultaneously, the hacker collective called the Electrohippies (ehippies) targeted the computer network servicing the WTO meeting. Furthermore, it was not just a small group of hackers aligning themselves with a larger movement per se but "with 450,000 people (or technically computers) participating over five days (Electrohippies Collective 2000)".[1]

It does, however, seem that so far neither the Palestinian hacktivist movement in the digital sphere nor the Palestinian social grassroots movements in the physical sphere are interested in such a thing.

PALESTINIAN HACKTIVISM AND THE TRANSGRESSION OF BORDERS

When #OpIsrael emerged as a response to the Israeli attack on the Gaza Strip, Operation Pillar of Defense, a video was published by the user *Hiluxanon* on YouTube, 17 November 2012, where Anonymous declared that it would launch the operation as a response to the Israelis' actions.[2] The campaign, which started in April 2013, implemented, among others, the use of DDoS attacks, database and information leaks and defacements. Among some of the Israeli websites targeted were those of the IDF, Israel Ministry of Defense and the Israeli prime minister.[3]

Furthermore, as regards hacktivism and border transgression, they used the slogans/motto of the initially Western-based Anonymous ("Expect us") and its logo, #OpIsrael, was represented by a large group of different Arab hacktivist groups such as Mauritanian Hacker Team, Moroccan Hackerz, Gaza Hacker Team, Gaza Security Team, Muslim Liberation Army and Algerian hackers, to mention a few.[4]

There are several examples where hackers throughout the world have joined together across borders in joint operations, such as Anonymous with members from Europe, Latin America, the United States and the rest of the world. #OpIsrael is in this regard a continuation of this development where it is not defined by solely Arab hackers or solely Western hackers, but rather that both groups cooperate across borders and continents against Israel. Thus, there are clear examples which show that the Internet in general and hacktivist campaigns in particular do transgress borders where the former enables qualitatively different groups in terms of geography, ideology and beliefs to cooperate on what they perceive as common causes.

Even Gaza Hacker Team, with its members (or rather affiliates) including a broad range of nationalities, epitomizes this border transgression: if one looks at the participants of the defacements in solidarity with Palestinian Islamic Jihad's Khaḍr ʿAdnān, there were, besides the Palestinian leadership of Gaza Hacker Team, thirteen other hackers that joined. Examples are the hacker "TKL" from Algeria (with the aforementioned avatar of Ibn Khattab),[5] "ehabneo" from Egypt,[6] "Mr_AnarShi-T" from Tunisia[7] and "mr.stalin" from Saudi Arabia.[8]

The first three hackers mentioned seem to be, or at least have been, regular participants who also joined the defacement protest campaign against the treatment of the al-Aqsa mosque mentioned earlier,[9] in addition to other non-Palestinian hackers such as "Black-Rose" from Egypt (who wrote the book on how to conduct SQL injection),[10] "Th-Mx" from Jordan,[11] "HANINE" from Lebanon,[12] "Micha"[13] and "zaradusht"[14] from Algeria and "aywanvictori"[15] and "llord"[16] from Morocco. Thus, it is evident that there is an actual, ongoing cooperation between Palestinian and non-Palestinian Arab hacktivists, where the latter contributes to the Palestinian resistance against Israel in cyberspace. All of the Arab hackers above, with the exception of llord, aywanvictory and mr.stalin, are labeled as either members or moderators of Gaza Hacker Team's internet forum.

As mr.leon himself commented, "If there is anything certain it is that the Internet made the world a small village",[17] and "But the most important aspect is that it [the Internet] has gathered the Arab and global hackers in targeting and taking advantage of their expertise in our attacks, and thus delivering a message".[18]

Hacktivism's internationalizing feature, then, might make us ask if electronic jihad is a rather more pan-Arab than Palestinian phenomenon. For example, AnonGhost, Syrian Electronic Army and Oxomar have been mentioned in this book for hacking Israeli cyber-infrastructure from abroad, and there is no doubt that pan-Arabism or pan-Islamism plays a role. Yet it does not overshadow the fact that purely Palestinian hacktivist teams have emerged, which conduct hacking as Palestinians and with a Palestinian-nationalist view. The hacktivist transgression of borders enabled by the Internet, with several international teams cooperating during events such as OpIsrael, has blurred these divisions, yet not obliterated them.

In terms of hacktivist action and campaigns transgressing borders, what does it mean, at least potentially? First of all, the hackings of Israel have had politico-religious effects, as the quotes from Suwaydan in the introduction show. As more and more Arab youths not only become interested but also directly involved in electronic jihad, it has become an issue for the religious scholars and authorities, the ulamā', in several Arab countries. The phenomenon has grown to such an extent that they have been forced to consider the legality of the digital means.

Though it is not unanimous, the majority is positive. For example, in 2008, with an increase of hacker activity against Israel and the United States and websites that were considered offensive to Islam, the Egyptian al-Azhar Fatwa Committee stated that "The mujāhid has the capacity of defending against aggression, and discipline the wrongdoers and oppressors. Hence, what has appeared across the Internet is the so-called 'electronic jihad' which is permissible in Islam".[19]

Furthermore, the issue spread to Morocco and the religious establishment there, as a hacker group calling themselves Moroccan Snipers hacked and defaced several Israeli websites with pictures of dead Palestinian children as a protest against Operation Cast Lead. The Moroccan ulamā' stated that the attacks on the Israeli websites were permissible in Islamic law and a part of electronic jihad.[20] Shaykh Bin Salim Basha, a member of the Moroccan ulamā', said it was "a real jihad", while Abu Zaid, another important Moroccan imam, stated "It is true there are laws that ban hacking and prohibit attacks on Internet sites, but they find themselves in a war situation against Israel and it's the right of Muslims to use every means, legal or illegal, to respond to the enemy".[21]

This is not to say that every Islamic scholar supports electronic jihad in general or the hacking of Israeli websites in particular, as was evident when a Saudi scholar, Shaykh Ṣāliḥ al-Fawzān, was asked by his student about its permissibility.[22] The student's question was:

Your eminence, Shaykh, some Muslims hack the websites of God's enemies among the Jews, Christians and others, and subsequently destroy them electronically, and damage the electronic content which leads to material and morale damages and injuries for the owners of these websites as they launch an electronic jihad. What is your opinion?

Ṣāliḥ al-Fawzān's fatwa and ruling on the question was:

This does not affect the infidels because they have the ability, means and innovations to fix what gets through, and then they will go and kill Muslims. So it is not permissible and it is useless for Muslims.

It is evident that al-Fawzān does not consider it a useful tool. You could in theory hack Israeli and other websites but it will not inflict any great damage, and the only thing that will result is their justification for revenging themselves by killing Muslims. Thus, hacktivism is, in spite of its noble intents, not permissible.

Yet what is interesting is not the fatwa itself, but how the Internet has led us to a situation where young Muslims, seeking guidance and answers to their questions, can cherry-pick from among a wide range of fatwas being published every single day, available to anyone connecting to the network – with many of the fatwas contradicting each other depending on the political and religious views of each scholar. When al-Fawzān's fatwa was broadcast in the news, it was republished on the Internet forum al-ghadīr, where he was ridiculed by its members, most likely youngsters. First shared by Ṭālib al-Masʿūdī, he wrote under the copied text: "Is it not truly astonishing that he worries about the hosts of the Jewish websites and their material losses? … Allah, save Islam and the Muslims from their [the ulamāʾ] evil and their fatwas."[23] Anwār 88 responded by saying al-Fawzān and the rest of the sheikhs were the "Sheikhs of treachery and ossification".[24]

In another forum, al-Quds Talk, the same news article was shared, causing the same indignation, while the user Islam simply stated "Do not bother. The ulamāʾ of the Sultans have been present in all times and places" and continued "Half a billion Muslims are afraid of four million Jews".[25] In countless forums you could read about the anger the fatwa produced, yet my point is to show how the Internet has given millions the opportunity, albeit under pseudonyms, to question and criticize the religious authority.

Secondly, on the issue of hacktivism and border transgression, we see that, with the hacktivist campaigns against Israel, local conflicts become further internationalized – which has been a continuous trend over the last decades. While conflict in the past was to a large degree interstate (the First World War involving soldiers killing each other in trenches and subsequently developing into total war with the Second World War), we saw with the Cold War how conflicts became intrastate: Civil wars between groups or between groups and regimes – often funded by regional or international hegemons. Of course, there are examples of extrastate conflicts, such as the conflict between international states and non-recognized states like the Islamic State.

So far, with the example of Israel/Palestine, hacktivism seems to be a continuation, or rather a diversification of the stakeholders of war where in the sphere of hacking and hacktivism we see the traditional: (1) *local/local*, but also (2) *international non-state/local*, (3) *local/international non-state*, and last but not least (4) *international non-state/international non-state*.

The first category of *local/local* stakeholders is what has been described here, the most elaborate in this book being Palestinian hackers attempting to penetrate the Israeli cyber-infrastructure and Israeli hackers, either non-state or within the Israeli military/intelligence, doing the same against Palestinian infrastructure.

Yet with foreign fighters hogging the headlines, and without any other comparison, the same internationalization applies to the sphere of hacktivism where the Internet's ability to transgress borders has enabled foreigners who are sitting miles away from the actual conflict and occupation to participate – in solidarity with Palestinians or because of personal ideological convictions independent of those involved on the ground. Syrian Electronic Army, Saudi Arabian Oxomar, the American Th3 J35t3r and several others that have been mentioned in this book fit the description of that development.

When it comes to the *local/international*, either state or non-state, this can be applied to both the Palestinian and Israeli spheres of hacktivism. Either where Palestinians have hacked foreign/international infrastructure to draw attention to the situation on the ground for the Palestinians under occupation, as was the case with KDMS Team, or Israeli hacktivist teams doing the same in, for example, Saudi Arabia, often as a response to earlier hacks conducted against Israeli firms or government agencies. However, Gaza Hacker Team's penetrations of cyber-infrastructure in, for example, Uganda and Burma, do not apply to this category as, while they are certainly examples of border transgression, they are not an internationalization of the Palestinian/Israeli conflict.

Perhaps most interesting is the category *international non-state/international non-state*, since we see, as regards hacktivism, how an initially local conflict suddenly involves two non-state actors, which theoretically do not have any geographical connection. The best example is the already mentioned Pakistani hacker Dr. Nuker, who hacked the Israeli lobby, AIPAC, publishing member information and credit card numbers. We have subsequently seen other international non-state actors hacking, or threatening to hack the websites of other states for their cooperation with Israel. One example is the hacktivist team AnonGhost, which threatened to attack the oil companies of Saudi Arabia and Kuwait for "acting in the interests of the United States and Israel".[26] Yet the subsequent attacks only resulted in a couple of websites being taken down by DDoS attacks.

The internationalization of conflicts within the sphere of hacktivism, and everything that it entails, raises some issues. On the one hand, hacktivism and border transgression involving both local and foreign actors is a symptom of the possibility-space where, as mr.leon stated, the world has, indeed, become a small village. This is not just in terms of my (hypothetical) personal ability to hack a website that could be miles away, but modern communications have made us involved, most often as observers, in what happens anywhere in the world – for example in Gaza. On the other hand, we should not forget that this development is not unidirectional, as the Palestinians themselves also necessarily get involved in completely different conflicts through news, social media and so on. This does explain Gaza Hacker Team's hacking of the Burmese websites in a conflict that enrages many more than just Muslims.

As I have discussed the ideological contradictions of Gaza Hacker Team, it is possible that the cooperation with other Muslim and Arab hackers across borders has hybridized their ideology. For example, it is possible that if Gaza Hacker Team only consisted of and participated with other Palestinian hackers, then their ideology would be more coherently nationalist. Yet with the cooperation with other Arab and Muslim hackers, Gaza Hacker Team has been forced to "adopt" more transnational terms and ideas in order to be, and function as, a joint platform for hackers from all over the Arab world with diverging convictions.

The conclusion is that Gaza Hacker Team is still a Palestinian phenomenon, but the border-transgressing nature of the Internet might have hybridized the team through its contact with other nationalities. Furthermore, it is precisely this transgressional nature that has forced the religious authorities to take a stand, as it has made it possible for men and women sitting thousands of miles away to hack cyber-infrastructure in Israel or any other part of the world.

DOES ELECTRONIC JIHAD MATTER?

The penetration of Israeli cyber-infrastructure has become globally diversified as it can be targeted from every single corner of the world – from Cape Town to Tromsø, from Tokyo to San Francisco. According to Erez Kreiner, former head of the Israeli National Information Security Authority, the rise of cyberattacks on Israel is considerable, but conducted by less professional elements "[a]ny future war Israel fights will involve massive attempts to hack Israel's computer and infrastructure networks". I have elaborated on hacktivism as a form of mimetic violence, and Kreiner emphasized that the attacks have created some public damage without hurting the Israeli state, but what worries him is a pinpointed, smart attack that goes under the radar: "The ability to harm us is there. It's just a matter of making the decision."[27]

Although Kreiner emphasized Israel's "exponentially better" cyber-defenses, some have, nevertheless, expressed the opinion that Israel is, in fact, more vulnerable than initially assessed. One of them is Tanya Attias, an Israeli cyber-intelligence consultant, who commented to *Haaretz*:

> We think we are a great cyber-secure nation, but we are
> kidding ourselves. What happened to Sony [the hacking
> of and information leak from Sony, November 2014,
> allegedly by North Korea], technically speaking, could
> happen here anytime. In fact, it already does. We just don't
> hear about it.[28]

However, we should not have the illusion that there is a power balance between the Palestinian hackers and the Israeli state. To compare the two would be to compare a modern industrial factory producing the Israeli Merkava tank to a home repair shop.

There is obviously a difference between the cyber-units of Hamas and Islamic Jihad, which get state funding in terms of money and equipment from Qatar, Iran and so on, and for example Gaza Hacker Team. Perhaps the two former will be able to penetrate the Israeli cyber-infrastructure in terms of what happened to Sony. As regards the hacktivist teams, such as Gaza Hacker Team, their strength might lie in quantity and not in quality. Hundreds of thousands or even millions of small-scale hacks annually conducted by hundreds of teams and individual hackers across the globe against Israeli firms, email users, credit cards and so on might do the trick.

I am not going to make that prediction. Yet I would simultaneously not assess Palestinian electronic jihad as a new "age" or period in the Palestinian resistance, as the fidā'ī, the shahīd or the istishhādī once were. It is too small, a parcel of Palestinian society, and has not made its mark on the Palestinian national narrative.

However, that does not mean that what the Palestinian hackers are doing is meaningless. Rather, as a part of the traditional Palestinian resistance, we should look at everything that the Palestinians do, from active and passive resistance, as one single entity. Each single feature of it that constitutes its wholeness, whether boycott, demonstrations, hacking or hunger strikes, will on its own seem weak; but connected and operating together they might be that decisive force of nature. For example, if one were to ask what boycotts or stone-throwing alone has achieved, the answer would be not so much. All of these methods together have, however, contributed immensely, from a situation in the 1960s when few had heard about the Palestinian struggle, to internationally organized BDS campaigns today.

If the future cyber-equivalent of the juggernaut will be conducted by a Palestinian, either inside Palestine or in the diaspora, the Middle East or any other place, is not certain, but what we do know is that:

> More than ever, this year has shown that taking up political disputes across international borders no longer requires planes, tanks and missiles. In a world where any man or woman behind a keyboard can become a soldier, the war over Palestine will no doubt rumble on long after the guns have been silenced.[29]

EPILOGUE

So what was Hamas and Egypt all about? And why was I so surprised? The thing is, yes, I did talk extensively with my sources in Hamas about Egypt, the Muslim Brotherhood, the coup d'état by Fatah al-Sisi and the SCAF, and how they felt it was proof that Islamic parties could not gain power because of the West and "their puppets" – as conversations usually do have some digressions.

Yet that part of the conversation was never written down, in articles, my master's thesis or in my book manuscript. It was only audio-taped and saved on my phone and computer – no one but me had access or knowledge of it. So how could the NNSA possibly know about it?

Perhaps they didn't, and I cannot say with certainty that they did know, but it seems very convenient that with a complete shot in the dark they would hit so perfectly on a question on Egypt and the Muslim Brotherhood of all things when my research and the topic of the interrogation was Palestinian hacktivism.

As I discussed the issue with sources in the Norwegian intelligence services – whether the Norwegian Intelligence Service

(E-tjenesten) could have hacked my phone or computer when I was in the West Bank – they stated that they doubted it, but the NNSA retained the right to question the Norwegian Police Security Service (PST) and foreign intelligence they cooperated with about me. As it is a poorly hidden secret that Norwegian intelligence is cooperating closely with Israeli intelligence, they could have got the tapes from them. In order to get to my point, we have to use some movie references.

The curious and even admirable thing about the James Bond film series is the way they portray what is deemed the main threat and challenge of the day. Whereas, initially, the Soviet Union or its spies more than once were the antagonists in the movies, the latest Bond movie, *Spectre*, magnificently illustrates one of the biggest concerns of today: encompassing surveillance. You know surveillance has gone too far when it creates problems for 007. Sadly, if I may digress, this is in addition to the fact that James Bond must be the worst spy in history as he tells everyone his actual name at first encounter.

In other words, as described in the introduction, we have come to a point in history where no information that we keep is safe. What we store on our computers, phones or most any electronic device seems to be open to whatever surveillance is out there. It was masterfully reflected by the main antagonist, Valentine, in the movie *Kingsman: The Secret Service* when he stated: "Know what I love about pen and paper? Nobody can hack into this shit."

But then again, storing everything as handwritten notes does not seem feasible, at least not if borders are to be crossed, such as the Israeli/Palestinian ones, where they are rather thorough when they check your luggage. And that would only be the case if this was applicable to Palestine. But as students and researchers are going to Africa, Latin America, Asia and every single place on earth where there is some kind of opposition which can be violently struck down, where protestors and activists are facing imprisonment or worse, we have realized that we are not able to keep them safe no matter what we do.

Yes, we can take precautions, but that is not enough. If Israeli intelligence, or anyone else for that matter, really wants to find them, they will.

At the master's level in our methodology classes we learned about post-colonialism, how to write a good project description, and about the ethical dilemmas we might face when we conducted our fieldwork, we never learned for a second about how to protect our sources in the world we actually work in: technological and all-encompassing surveillance.

Perhaps universities all over the world need to have methodology classes where master's and doctoral students are taught about basic encryption, proxy servers and the like. To believe it would completely secure all of our sources would be naïve, but the situation today cannot even be compared to that of not having a lock for your door. It would be more apt to say that our homes do not even have a front door installed, with lit arrows pointing out that everyone who would like to do so can enter.

It is an essential task not limited to academia and journalists, but a task for society at large to stop the surveillance which no one would possibly believe is limited to the issue of security. It is urgent. As professor in computer science at the University of California Phillip Rogaway writes in the abstract to the paper "The

Moral Character of Cryptographic Work", which should be quoted in its entirety:

> Cryptography rearranges power: It configures who can do what, from what. This makes cryptography an inherently *political* tool, and it confers on the field an intrinsically *moral* dimension. The Snowden revelations motivate a reassessment of the political and moral positioning of cryptography. They lead one to ask if our inability to effectively address mass surveillance constitutes a failure of our field. I believe that it does. I call for a community-wide effort to develop more effective means to resist mass surveillance.[1]

To modify the quote from Kevin Kelly given in the introduction, as we can look back on what actually has happened: "No one has been more right about computerization than George Orwell in *1984*. So far, nearly everything about the actual possibility-space that computers have created indicates they are the beginning and implementation of overall authority and surveillance."[2]

NOTES

INTRODUCTION

1. Lappin, Y. (2012) "Anti-Israel hackers strike El Al, TASE websites" (on net), 16 January, http://www.jpost.com/National-News/Anti-Israel-hackers-strike-El-Al-TASE-websites [accessed: 10 October 2015].

2. Al-Iqtisadiyya (2012) "al-Hākkir ʿOxomar' yanshuru mazīdan min baṭāqāt al-iʾtimān al-isrāʾīliyya" (on net), 12 January, http://www.aleqt.com/2012/01/12/article_615664.html [accessed: 8 October 2015].

3. Ibid.: "Adʿū al-hākkirz al-ʿarab al-muslimīn li-al-tawaḥḥud ḍidd Isrāʾīl wa al-inḍ imām li-hadhihi al-ḥarb kamā adʿū al-hākkirz al-atrāk alladīn yakhtaraqūn al-ʿadīd min al-mawāqiʿ al-iliktrūniyya yawmiyyan" (Translation: "I urge all Muslim and Arab hackers to unite against Israel and join this war, as well as all Turkish hackers who attack the websites daily").

4. al-Jazeera (2012) "Qarāṣina isrāʾīliyyūn yuridūn ʿalā al-ʿarab" (on net), 18 January http://goo.gl/vjLnC9 [accessed: 7 April 2016]. .

5. Mikelberg, A. (2012) "Israeli government vows to catch Saudi hacker teen who published thousands of credit card numbers, personal data" (on net), 9 January, http://www.nydailynews.com/news/world/israeli-government-vows-catch-saudi-hacker-teen-published-thousands-credit-card-numbers-personal-data-article-1.1003655 [accessed: 9 October 2015].

6. Deger, A. (2012) "Saudi hacker plays cat-n-mouse with oh-so serious foreign minister" (on net), 17 January, http://mondoweiss.net/2012/01/saudi-hacker-interviewed-on-game-of-cat-and-mouse-with-israel [accessed: 9 October 2015].

7. Dotson, K. (2012) "Israel vs. Saudi Arabia hacks heating up as Israeli hackers respond in kind" (on net), 18 January, http://siliconangle.com/blog/2012/01/18/israel-vs-saudi-arabia-hacks-heating-up-as-israeli-hackers-respond-in-kind/ [accessed: 9 October 2015].

8. Donia al-Watan (2012) "'Malik al-ḥākkir al-saʿūdī' ... fī dhimmat Allāh" ["The Saudi-Arabian hacker king" ... in the protection of God] (on net), 21 April, http://www.alwatanvoice.com/arabic/news/2012/04/21/271892.html [accessed: 12 October 2015].

9. Memri TV (2011) "#2980 – Kuwaiti Islamist preacher Tareq Sweidan, manager of Resala TV, calls for armed resistance and Electronic Jihad against Israel" (on net), 04 June, http://www.memritv.org/clip/en/2980.htm Transcription part 01:56–02:33: "Wa anna hunāk shayʾ ism jihād iʿlāmī wa hunāk shayʾ ism jihād siyāsī, wa hunāk shayʾ an adʿū al-shabāb bi-shadda lahu alān anā arjaʿ an yabdaʾ jihād iliktrūnī [...] hādhā ʿandī aḥsan min ʿashrīn ʿamaliyya jihādiyya..." [accessed: 11 October 2015].

10. Suwaydan, T. (2012) "Arā ḍarūrat tajmīʿ juhūd al-ḥakkirz fī mashrūʿ al-jihād al-iliktrūnī ḍidd al-ʿaddū al-ṣahyūnī wa huwwa jihād fiʿāl wa muhimm wa ajruhu ʿaẓīm bi-idhn Allāh" [Twitter], 17 January, https://twitter.com/TareqAlSuwaidan/status/159363852956475392 [accessed: 8 October 2015].

11. Trendle, G. (2002) "Cyberwar". *The World Today*, vol. 58 (4), p. 7.

12. McChesney, R. (2013) *Digital Disconnect: How Capitalism is Turning the Internet Against Democracy*. New York, London: The New Press, p. 97.

13. Quoted in: Thornton, A. L. (2001) "Does the Internet create democracy?" *Ecquid Novi: African Journalism Studies*, vol. 22 (2), p. 128.

14. McChesney, R. (2013) *Digital Disconnect: How Capitalism is Turning the Internet Against Democracy*. New York, London: The New Press, p. 97.

15. Kelly, K. (1996) "The Electronic Hive: Embrace It". In: Kling. R. (ed.) *Computerization and Controversy: Value Conflicts and Social Changes*. San Diego, San Francisco, New York, Boston, London, Sydney, Tokyo: Morgan Kaufmann, p. 78.

16. McChesney, R. (2013) *Digital Disconnect: How Capitalism is Turning the Internet Against Democracy*. New York, London: The New Press, p. 102.

17. Samuel, A. W. (2004) *Hacktivism and the Future of Political Participation*. PhD thesis, Cambridge, Massachusetts: Harvard University, p. 102.

18. Jordan, T. & Taylor, P. A. (2004) *Hacktivism and Cyberwars: Rebels with a Cause?* New York, London: Routledge Taylor & Francis Group, p. 12.

19. Ibid.

20. Ibid., p. 15.

21. Ibid., p. 16.

22. Ibid., p. 17.

23. Vegh, S. (2002) "Hacktivism or cyberterrorism? The changing media discourse on hacking" (on net). *First Monday: Peer-reviewed Journal on the Internet*, vol. 7, (7), http://firstmonday.org/article/view/998/919

24. Jordan, T. & Taylor, P. A. (2004) *Hacktivism and Cyberwars: Rebels with a Cause?* New York, London: Routledge Taylor & Francis Group, p. 98.

25. Apps, Peter (2010) "Analysis: WikiLeaks battle: a new amateur face of cyber war?" (on net), 9 December, http://www.reuters.com/article/2010/12/09/us-wikileaks-cyberwarfare-amateur-idUSTRE6B81K520101209 [accessed: 11 October 2015].

26. Jordan, T. & Taylor, P. A. (2004) *Hacktivism and Cyberwars: Rebels with a Cause?* New York, London: Routledge Taylor & Francis Group, p. 69.

27. Andress, J. & Winterfeld, S. (2011) *Cyber Warfare. Techniques, Tactics and Tools for Security Practicioners.* Amsterdam, Boston, London, New York, Oxford, Paris, San Diego, Singapore, Sydney, Tokyo: Elsevier Syngress.

1. THE RESISTANCE DEVELOPS

1. Wood, E. M. (2008) *Citizens to Lords: A Social History of Western Political Thought from Antiquity to the Late Middle Ages.* London, New York: Verso Books, p. 4.

2. See for example: Morris, B. (2004) "In '48, Israel did what it had to do" (on net), 26 January, http://articles.latimes.com/2004/jan/26/opinion/oe-morris26 [accessed: 12 October 2015]; and Pappé, I. (2007) *The Ethnic Cleansing of Palestine.* Oxford: Oneworld Publications.

3. Waage, H. H. (2013) *Konflikt og Stormaktspolitikk i Midtøsten.* Kristiansand: Cappelen Damm Akademisk, p. 170.

4. Abufarha, N. (2009) *The Making of a Human Bomb. An Ethnography of Palestinian Resistance.* Durham, London: Duke University Press, p. 44.

5. For a more elaborate analysis of the development from the fidā'ī into the shahīd and subsequently into the istishhādī see: ibid.

6. Ibid., p. 47.

7. Fanon, F. (2001) *The Wretched of the Earth.* London: Penguin Books, p. 28.

8. Tveit, O. K. (2015) *De skyldige.* Oslo: Kagge Forlag, p. 23.

9. Fruchter-Ronen, I. (2008) "Black September: the 1970–71 events and their impact on the formation of Jordanian national identity". *Civil Wars*, vol. 10 (3), p. 247.

10. Tveit, O. K. (2015) *De skyldige.* Oslo: Kagge Forlag, p. 70–71.

11. Fruchter-Ronen, I. (2008) "Black September: the 1970–71 events and their impact on the formation of Jordanian national identity". *Civil Wars*, vol. 10 (3), pp. 249–250.

12. Quoted in: Massad, J. A. (2006) *The Persistence of the Palestinian Question: Essays on Zionism and the Palestinians.* Abingdon, Oxon: Routledge, p. 33.

13. Ibid.

14. Quoted in: Schindler, C. (2008) *A History of Modern Israel.* New York: Cambridge University Press, p. 153.

15. Quoted in: Ubaysiri, K. (2004) "Virtual hostage dramas and real politics". *Ejournalist*, vol. 4 (2), p. 4.

16. Žižek, S. (2009) *Violence: Six Sideways Reflections.* London: Profile Books Ltd., p. 2.

17. As narrated in: Ibid., p. 9.

2. THE SHAHĪD AND THE NORMALIZATION OF OCCUPATION

1. See for example: Fukuyama, F. (2006) *The End of History and the Last Man.* New York: Free Press.

2. Høigilt, J. (2013) "The Palestinian Spring that was not: the youth and political activism in the occupied Palestinian territories". *Arab Studies Quarterly*, vol. 35 (4), p. 346.

3. Abufarha, N. (2009) *The Making of a Human Bomb. An Ethnography of Palestinian Resistance.* Durham, London: Duke University Press, p. 60.

4. Coulter, J. (1998) "Why I am not a right-winger: a response to David Horowitz". *New Political Science*, vol. 20 (1), p. 102.

5. Laub, Z. (2014) "Hamas" (on net), 1 January, http://www.cfr.org/israel/hamas/p8968 [accessed: 12 October 2015].

6. Schanzer, J. (2008) *Hamas vs. Fatah: The Struggle for Palestine.* New York: Palgrave Macmillan, p. 42.

7. Jean-Klein, I. (2003) "Into committees, out of the house? Familiar forms in the organization of Palestinian committee activism during the first intifada". *American Ethnologists*, vol. 30 (4), p. 557.

8. King, M. E. (2007) *A Quiet Revolution: The First Palestinian Intifada and Nonviolent Resistance.* New York: Nation Books, p. 2.

9. Hass, A. (2013) "The inner syntax of Palestinian stone-throwing" (on net), 3 April, http://www.haaretz.com/opinion/the-inner-syntax-of-palestinian-stone-throwing.premium-1.513131?date=1445241507019 [accessed: 19 October 2015].

10. Darweish, M. & Rigby, A. (2015) *Popular Protest in Palestine: The Uncertain Future of Unarmed Resistance.* London: Pluto Press, pp. 60–62.

11. Quoted in: ibid., p. 78.

12. Schiocchet, L. (2011) "Palestinian Sumud: steadfastness, ritual and time among Palestinian refugees". Birzeit University Working Paper 2011/51, Migration and Refugee Module, p. 1.

13. Rijke, A. & van Teeffelen, T. (2014) "To exist is to resist: Sumud, heroism, and the everyday". *Jerusalem Quarterly*, issue 59, p. 86.
14. Darweish, M. & Rigby, A. (2015) *Popular Protest in Palestine: The Uncertain Future of Unarmed Resistance*. London: Pluto Press, p. 57.
15. Ibid., p. 40.
16. Ibid., p. 41.
17. Parker, S. (2014) *Bertolt Brecht: A Literary Life*. London, New Delhi, New York, Sydney: Bloomsbury, p. 385.

3. A DIGITAL FORTRESS: THE ISRAELI MILITARY–DIGITAL COMPLEX

1. Who Is Hosting This? (2014) "Internet censorship around the globe" (on net), 20 February, http://www.whoishostingthis.com/blog/2014/02/20/Internet-censorship/ [accessed: 13 October 2015].
2. Hofheinz, A. (2005) "The Internet in the Arab world: playground for political liberalization". Internationale Politik und Gesellschaft, issue 3, p. 80.
3. Vincent, P. & Warf, B (2007) "Multiple Geographies of the Arab Internet". *Area*, vol. 1, p. 90.
4. The Economist (2014) "Surfing the shabaka" (on net), 12 April, http://www.economist.com/news/middle-east-and-africa/21600732-worlds-fifth-most-spoken-language-lags-online-surfing-shabaka [accessed: 13 October 2015].
5. Vincent, P. & Warf, B (2007) "Multiple geographies of the Arab Internet". *Area*, vol. 39 (1), p. 88.
6. Wheeler, D. L. (2009) "Working around the Arab state: Internet use and political identity in the Arab world". In: Chadwick, A. & Howard, P. N. (eds.) *Routledge Handbook of Internet Politics*. New York: Routledge, p. 307.
7. Wheeler, D. L. (2006) "Empowering publics: information technology and democratization in the Arab world – lessons from Internet cafés and beyond". Oxford Internet Institute, Research Report no. 11, p. 6.
8. ICT Facts and Figures (2013) *The World in 2013*. ICT Data and Statistics Division, p. 3.
9. Wheeler, D. L. (2009) "Working around the Arab state: Internet use and political identity in the Arab world". In: Chadwick, A. & Howard, P. N. (eds.) *Routledge Handbook of Internet Politics*. New York: Routledge, p. 311.
10. Ibid.
11. Hofheinz, A. (2011) "Nextopia? Beyond revolution 2.0". *International Journal of Communication*, vol. 5, p. 1418.
12. Tufekci, Z. & Wilson, C. (2012) "Social media and the decision to participate in political protest: observations from Tahrir Square". *Journal of Communication*, vol. 62 (1), p. 365.

13. Ibid., p. 376.

14. Wheeler, D. L. (2006) "Empowering publics: information technology and democratization in the Arab world – lessons from Internet cafés and beyond". Oxford Internet Institute, Research Report no. 11, p. 17.

15. The RSA (2011) "The Internet in society: empowering or censoring citizens?" [YouTube], 14 March, https://www.youtube.com/watch?v=Uk8x3V-sUgU [accessed: 18 November 2015], 8:40–8:58.

16. The Event is one of the best-known and most important theories of the French philosopher Alain Badiou, and is in many ways an extension of Maoism and its theory of revolution. Andrew Robinson describes it thus: "In an Event, the inconsistent multiplicity which always lies beneath a particular social order is able to appear subjectively. Only in an Event can the excluded part be visible. An Event succeeds in representing a part which is previously unrepresented. This unfolding of new representations from an Event produces Truths, Subjects, and new social systems." (Robinson, A. (2014) "An A to Z of theory | Alain Badiou: the event" (on net), 15 December, https://ceasefiremagazine.co.uk/alain-badiou-event/ [accessed: 5 April 2016].

17. The RSA (2011) "The Internet in society: empowering or censoring citizens?" [YouTube], 14 March, https://www.youtube.com/watch?v=Uk8x3V-sUgU [accessed: 18 November 2015], 7:35–7:57.

18. Carmel, E. & de Fontenay, C. (2001) "Israel's Silicon Wadi: the forces behind cluster formation". SIEPR Discussion Paper 00-40. Stanford University (June), p. 2.

19. Eisenhower, D. D. (n.d.) "Military-industrial complex speech, Dwight D. Eisenhower, 1961" (on net), http://coursesa.matrix.msu.edu/~hst306/documents/indust.html [accessed: 13 October 2015].

20. Derouen Jr., K. (2000) "The guns–growth relationship in Israel". *Journal of Peace Research*, vol. 37 (1), p. 73.

21. Lysestøl, P. M. (2016) *Israel Bak Muren av Myter og Propaganda*. Oslo: Forlaget Manifest, pp. 95, 96 and 107.

22. Ibid., p. 108.

23. Ibid., p. 94.

24. Derouen Jr., K. (2000) "The guns–growth relationship in Israel". *Journal of Peace Research*, vol. 37 (1), p. 75.

25. Lysestøl, P. M. (2016) *Israel Bak Muren av Myter og Propaganda*. Oslo: Forlaget Manifest, p. 96.

26. Hanieh, A. (2003) "From state-led growth to globalization: the evolution of Israeli capitalism". *Journal of Palestine Studies*, vol. 32 (4), p. 14.

27. Halper, J. (2015) *The War Against the People: Israel, the Palestinians and Global Pacification*. London: Pluto Press, p. 266.

28. Derouen Jr., K. (2000) "The Guns-Growth Relationship in Israel". In: *Journal of Peace Research*, vol. 37 (1), p. 79/80.

29. Bichler, S. & Nitzan, J. (1995) "The great U-turn: restructuring in Israel and South Africa". *New From Within*, vol. 11 (9), p. 29.

30. Ibid., p. 30.

31. See for example: Fukuyama, F. (2006) *The End of History and the Last Man*. New York: Free Press.

32. Quoted in: Halper, J. (2015) *The War Against the People: Israel, the Palestinians and Global Pacification*. London: Pluto Press, p. 258 (italics added).

33. Ibid., p. 259.

34. Bichler, S. & Nitzan, J. (2002) "The new economy or transnational ownership? The global policy economy of Israel" [Conference Paper]. In: *The Regional Divide: Promises and Realities of the New Economy in a Transatlantic Perspective*. Toronto, Canada (3–4 May), p. 60.

35. Lysestøl, P. M. (2016) *Israel Bak Muren av Myter og Propaganda*. Oslo: Forlaget Manifest, pp. 128–129.

36. Bichler, S. & Nitzan, J. (2002) "The new economy or transnational ownership? The global policy economy of Israel" [Conference Paper]. In: *The Regional Divide: Promises and Realities of the New Economy in a Transatlantic Perspective*. Toronto, Canada (3–4 May), p. 60; and Lysestøl, P. M. (2016) *Israel Bak Muren av Myter og Propaganda*. Oslo: Forlaget Manifest, p. 124.

37. Hanieh, A. (2003) "From state-led growth to globalization: the evolution of Israeli capitalism". *Journal of Palestine Studies*, vol. 32 (4), p. 14.

38. Who Profits/The Coalition of Women for Peace (2011) *Technologies of Control: The Case of Hewlett Packard*. Tel Aviv: Yegia Kapayim St, p. 7.

39. Halper, J. (2015) *The War Against the People: Israel, the Palestinians and Global Pacification*. London: Pluto Press, p. 266.

40. Ibid., p. 105.

41. Carmel, E. & de Fontenay, C. (2001) Israel's Silicon Wadi: the forces behind cluster formation. SIEPR Discussion Paper 00-40. Stanford University (June), p. 5.

42. Ibid., p. 9.

43. Ibid., p. 10.

44. Butler, J. S. & Swed, O. (2015) "Military capital in the Israeli hi-tech industry". *Armed Forces & Societies*, vol. 41 (1), p. 124.

45. Ibid., pp. 127–129.

46. Carmel, E. & de Fontenay, C. (2001) Israel's Silicon Wadi: the forces behind cluster formation. SIEPR Discussion Paper 00-40. Stanford University (June), p. 27.

47. Ibid., p. 27.

48. Halper, J. (2015) *The War Against the People: Israel, the Palestinians and Global Pacification*. London: Pluto Press, p. 267.

49. Neuman, E. (2014) "Israel's army, a high-tech powerhouse without the sense to cash in" (on net), 13 August, http://www.haaretz.com/business/.premium-1. 610148 [accessed: 13 October 2015].

50. Ibid.

51. Ein-Dor, P. Goodman, S. E. & Wolcott, P. (2000) "From Via Maris to electronic highway: the Internet in Canaan". *Communications of the ACM*, vol. 43 (7), p. 20.

52. Vincent, P. & Warf, B. (2007) "Multiple geographies of the Arab Internet". *Area*, vol. 1, p. 93.

53. Ein-Dor, P. Goodman, S. E. & Wolcott, P. (2000) "From Via Maris to electronic highway: the Internet in Canaan". *Communications of the ACM*, vol. 43 (7), p. 21.

54. Ma'an News Agency (2013) "3G void limits West Bank's smartphone revolution" (on net), 24 July, http://www.maannews.com/Content.aspx?id=616583 [accessed: 13 October 2015].

55. Personal communication (anecdotal/experiential evidence), Ramallah, 9 September 2014.

56. Arafeh, N., Abdullah, W. F. & Bahour, S. (2015) "ICT: The shackled engine of Palestine's Development" (on net), 9 November, https://al-shabaka.org/briefs/ict-the-shackled-engine-of-palestines-development/ [accessed: 19 April 2015].

57. Nashif, N. (2016) "Israel-Palestine: social media as a tool of oppression"(on net), 18 April, http://www.huffingtonpost.com/nadim-nashif/israel-palestine-social-media_b_9699816.html [accessed: 19 April 2015].

58. Prusher, I. R. (1996) "Palestinians sprint to break Israeli grip on phone lines" (on net), 20 August, http://www.csmonitor.com/1996/0820/082096.intl. intl.2.html [accessed: 13 October 2015]

59. Vincent, P. & Warf, B. (2007) "Multiple geographies of the Arab Internet". *Area*, vol. 1, p. 84.

60. Internet World Stats (n.d.) "Palestine Territory (Gaza and West Bank) Internet usage, broadband and telecommunication reports" (on net), http://www. Internetworldstats.com/me/ps.htm [accessed: 13 October 2015].

61. Bates, T. R. (1975) "Gramsci and the theory of hegemony". *Journal of the History of Ideas*, vol. 36 (2), p. 351.

62. Aouragh, M. (2008) "Everyday resistance on the Internet: the Palestinian context". *Journal of Arab and Muslim Media Research*, vol. 1 (2), p. 115.

63. Counter-publics are in this book defined as by Nancy Fraser: "parallel discursive arenas where members of subordinated social groups invent and circulate counterdiscourses, which in turn permits them to formulate oppositional

interpretations of their identities, interests and needs". Fraser, N. (1990), "Rethinking the public sphere: a contribution to the critique of actually existing democracy". *Social Text*, no. 25/26 , p. 67.

4. THE ISTISHHĀDĪ AND THE EMERGENCE OF PALESTINIAN ELECTRONIC JIHAD

1. Allen, L. (2008) "Getting by the occupation: how violence became normal during the Second Palestinian Intifada". *Cultural Anthropology*, vol. 23 (3), p. 455.
2. Pressman, J. (2003) "The Second Intifada: background and causes of the Israeli–Palestinian conflict". *The Journal of Conflict Studies*, vol. 23 (2), https://journals.lib.unb.ca/index.php/jcs/article/view/220/378 [accessed: 19 November 2015].
3. Halper, J. (2015) *The War Against the People: Israel, the Palestinians and Global Pacification*. London: Pluto Press, p. 174.
4. Abufarha, N. (2009) *The Making of a Human Bomb. An Ethnography of Palestinian Resistance*. Durham, London: Duke University Press, p. 78.
5. Ibid., p. 77.
6. Ibid., p. 158.
7. Darweish, M. & Rigby, A. (2015) *Popular Protest in Palestine: The Uncertain Future of Unarmed Resistance*. London: Pluto Press, p. 68.
8. Quoted in Tuastad, D. (2003) "Neo-Orientalism and the new barbarism thesis: aspects of symbolic violence in the Middle East conflict(s)". *Third World Quarterly*, vol. 24 (4), p. 596.
9. Gregory, D. (2004) "Palestine and the 'War on Terror'". *Comparative Studies of South Asia, Africa and the Middle East*, vol. 24 (1), p. 184.
10. Quoted in: ibid.
11. Harel, A. (2006) "Shin Bet: Palestinian truce main cause for reduced terror" (on net), 1 February, http://www.haaretz.com/print-edition/news/shin-bet-palestinian-truce-main-cause-for-reduced-terror-1.61607 [accessed: 14 October 2015].
12. Newton, M. (2004) *Hich-Tech Crime and Crime-Fighting: From Airport Security to the ZYX Computer virus*. New York: Checkmark Books, p. 308.
13. Ibid.
14. A mirror site is a copy of an existing website, and is set up in order to reduce network traffic.
15. Newton, M. (2004) *High-Tech Crime and Crime-Fighting: From Airport Security to the ZYX Computer Virus*. New York: Checkmark Books, p. 308.
16. Allen, P. D. & Demchak, C. C. (2003) "The Palestinian–Israeli: cyberwar". *Military Review*, vol. 83 (2), p. 52.

17. Gambill, G. C. (2000) "Who's winning the Arab–Israeli cyber war?" *Middle East Intelligence Bulletin*, vol. 2, November (10).

18. Ibid.

19. Ibid.

20. Hershman, T. (2001) "Israeli discusses the 'inter-fada'" (on net), 12 January, http://archive.wired.com/politics/law/news/2001/01/41154 [accessed: 14 October 2015].

21. Halper, J. (2015) *The War Against the People: Israel, the Palestinians and Global Pacification*. London: Pluto Press, p. 106.

22. Krebs, B. (2013) "DHS: 'OpUSA' may be more bark than bite" (on net), 2 May, http://krebsonsecurity.com/2013/05/dhs-opusa-may-be-more-bark-than-bite/ [accessed: 14 October 2015].

23. Palestine National Authority/Palestinian Central Bureau of Statistics (2008) *Palestine in Figures 2007*. Ramallah, Palestine: Palestinian Central Bureau of Statistics, p. 8.

24. Ibid.

25. Ibid., p. 17.

26. Ibid., p. 8.

27. International Business Publications, USA (2015) *Palestine (West Bank and Gaza) Education System and Policy Handbook, volume 1 Strategic Information and Developments*. Washington, DC: Global Investment Center, USA, p. 55.

28. Ibid.

29. Gambetta, D. & Hertog, S. (2007) *Engineers of Jihad* (on net). Sociology Working Papers, Paper Number 2007-10, Department of Sociology, University of Oxford, Oxford OX1 3UQ, http://www.sociology.ox.ac.uk/materials/papers/2007-10.pdf, p. 34.

30. Ibid., p. 12.

31. Quoted in: Farwell, J. P. & Rohozinski, R. (2011) "Stuxnet and the future of cyber war". *Survival*, vol. 53 (1), p. 23.

32. Langner, R. (2011) "Stuxnet: dissecting a cyberwarfare weapon". *Security and Privacy, IEEE*, vol. 9 (3), p. 49.

33. Kelley, M. B. (2013) "The Stuxnet attack on Iran's nuclear plant was 'far more dangerous' than previously thought" (on net), 20 November, http://www.businessinsider.com/stuxnet-was-far-more-dangerous-than-previous-thought-2013-11 [accessed: 19 October 2015].

34. Haaretz (2013) "Snowden says Israel, U.S. created Stuxnet virus that attacked Iran" (on net), 9 July, http://www.haaretz.com/news/diplomacy-defense/1.534728 [accessed: 15 October 2015].

35. Nakashima, E. & Warrick, J. (2012) "Stuxnet was work of U.S. and Israeli experts, officials say" (on net), 2 June, https://www.washingtonpost.com/

world/national-security/stuxnet-was-work-of-us-and-israeli-experts-officials-say/2012/06/01/gJQAlnEy6U_story.html [accessed: 15 October 2015].

36. Farwell, J. P. & Rohozinski, R. (2011) "Stuxnet and the future of cyber war". *Survival*, vol. 53 (1), p. 30.

37. Halper, J. (2015) *The War Against the People: Israel, the Palestinians and Global Pacification*. London: Pluto Press, p. 107.

5. GAZA HACKER TEAM: ELECTRONIC JIHADISTS AND SCRIPT KIDDIES

1. Shamah, D. (2012) "How Israel police computers were hacked: the inside story" (on net), 28 October, http://www.timesofisrael.com/how-israel-police-computers-were-hacked-the-inside-story/ and Haq, T., Moran, N. & Villeneuve, N. (2013) "Operation Molerats: Middle East cyber attacks using Poison Ivy" (on net), 23 October, https://www.fireeye.com/blog/threat-research/2013/08/operation-molerats-middle-east-cyber-attacks-using-poison-ivy.html [both accessed: 23 October 2015].

2. Shamah, D. (2014) "Xtreme RAT bites Israeli government sites, yet again" (on net), 12 February, http://www.timesofisrael.com/xtreme-rat-bites-israeli-government-sites-yet-again/ [accessed: 23 October 2015].

3. Haq, T., Moran, N. & Villeneuve, N. (2013) "Operation Molerats: Middle East cyber attacks using Poison Ivy" (on net), 23 October ,https://www.fireeye.com/blog/threat-research/2013/08/operation-molerats-middle-east-cyber-attacks-using-poison-ivy.html [accessed: 23 October 2015].

4. mr.leon, personal communication, 10 March 2015.

5. Ibid., 10 September 2014: "Lā nantamī ilā ayy ḥaraka … Naḥnu shabāb falasṭīniyyīn min Ghazza" [We do not belong to any movement… We are Palestinian youth from Gaza].

6. Personal communication (anecdotal/experiential evidence), 27 September 2014.

7. The Internet Wayback Machine (2014) "Gaza Hacker Team forum, frontpage" (on net), 26 June, https://web.archive.org/web/20140626165239/http://gaza-hacker.net/cc/ [accessed: 23 October 2015].

8. Gaza Youth Breaks Out (n.d.) "Manifesto 1.0", http://gazaybo.wordpress.com/manifesto-0-1/ [accessed: 23 October 2015].

9. Personal communication (anecdotal/experiential evidence).

10. Skare, E. (2013) "Norman Finkelstein om Oslo-avtalen, palestinsk quisling-styre og intifadaen" (on net), 11 January, http://radikalportal.no/2013/01/11/norman-finkelstein-om-oslo-avtalen-palestinsk-quislingstyre-og-intifadaen/ [accessed: 24 October 2015].

11. Word By Map (2014) "Median age" (on net), 13 April, http://world.bymap. org/MedianAge.html [accessed: 23 October 2015].

12. Høigilt, J. (2013) "The Palestinian Spring that was not: the youth and political activism in the occupied Palestinian territories". *Arab Studies Quarterly*, vol. 35 (4), p. 350.

13. Quoted in: Žižek, S. (2009) *Violence: Six Sideways Reflections*. London: Profile Books, pp. 32–33.

14. Syrian Electronic Army, personal communication, 31 March 2015.

15. mr.leon, personal communication, 15 September 2014: "nu'tabir juz'a min al-muqāwama al-falasṭīniyya al-musallaḥa" [We are a part of the Palestinian armed resistance].

16. Gaza Hacker Team (n.d.) "Mr.leon: Ma'lūmāt 'annī", http://gaza-hacker.net/ cc/member-u_9.html [accessed: 21 September 2014]. The website is no longer accessible.

17. Gaza Hacker Team (n.d.) "Casper: Ma'lūmāt 'annī", http://gaza-hacker.net/cc/ member-u_20.html [accessed: 21 September 2014]. The website is no longer accessible.

18. Gaza Hacker Team (n.d.) "ihdā' li-al-sha'b al-falasṭīnī: Injāzāt Farīq Qarāṣinat Ghazza" [A dedication to the Palestinian people: the achievements of Gaza Hacker Team], p. 5.

19. Ibid., p. 6, "fa-al-ḥasā'ir sanawiyyan taṣil ilā malāyyīn al-dūllārāt bi-sabbab 'amaliyyāt al-ikhtirāq wa nisaf al-mawāqi'" [So the yearly loss in the millions of dollars because of the hacker operations and destruction of websites].

20. mr.leon, personal communication, 29 September 2014: "fa-al-ikhtirāqāt taḍ urr bi-al-iqtiṣād al-isrā'īlī wa tu'aththir bi-shakl mubāshir 'alā iṣḥāb al-sharikāt al-istiḍāfa li-'adam thuqqat al-'umalā' bihim" ["so the attacks hurt the Israeli economy and affects the hosting companies directly due to the lack of customer confidence in them"].

21. InfoSecurity (2012) "DDoS and the collateral damage of hacktivism" (on net), 21 August, http://www.infosecurity-magazine.com/news/ddos-and-the-collat-eral-damage-of-hacktivism/ [accessed: 23 October 2015].

22. Ohlheiser, A. (2013) "Hackers shut down a tunnel road in Israel" (on net), 27 October, http://www.thewire.com/global/2013/10/hackers-shut-down-tunnel-road-israel/70983/ [accessed: 24 October 2015].

23. mr.leon, personal comment, 29 September 2014: "wa ayḍan īṣāl rasā'il 'alā wājihat al-mawāqi'" ["and it also sends a message on the websites"].

24. Ibid., p. 7.

25. al-Aqsa Martyrs' Brigade fighter, personal communication, 15 October 2014.

26. Main representative Palestinian Islamic Jihad West Bank, personal communi-cation, 16 November 2014.

27. Zitun, Y. (2012) "Cyber attacks didn't harm vital systems" (on net), 16 January, http://www.ynetnews.com/articles/0,7340,L-4176543,00.html [accessed: 23 October 2015].

28. Goldberg, M. (2012) "An eye for an eye a hack for a hack" (on net), 24 January, http://www.jpost.com/Blogs/Israel-up-close-and-personal/An-eye-for-an-eye-a-hack-for-a-hack-366176 [accessed: 23 October 2014].

29. Carl in Jerusalem (2012) "El Al and Tel Aviv Stock Exchange websites hacked" (on net), 16 January, http://israelmatzav.blogspot.no/2012/01/el-al-and-tel-aviv-stock-exchange.html [accessed: 23 October 2015].

30. Kerr, D. (2014) "Israel Army's Twitter account hacked, posts 'incorrect' tweets" (on net), 3 July, http://www.cnet.com/news/israel-armys-twitter-account-hacked-posts-incorrect-tweets/ [accessed: 23 October 2015].

31. Ibid.

32. Cohen, G. (2013) "IDF forms new force to combat cyber warfare" (on net), 4 March, http://www.haaretz.com/israel-news/idf-forms-new-force-to-combat-cyber-warfare.premium-1.506979 [accessed: 23 October 2015].

33. Prime Minister's Office (2014) "Decision to establish a new national authority for operative cyber defense" (on net), 21 September, http://www.pmo.gov.il/English/MediaCenter/Spokesman/Pages/spokecyber2210914.aspx [accessed: 23 October 2015].

34. Hill, K. (2013) "Here's what it looks like when a 'smart toilet' gets hacked [video]" (on net), 15 August, http://www.forbes.com/sites/kashmirhill/2013/08/15/heres-what-it-looks-like-when-a-smart-toilet-gets-hacked-video/ [accessed: 23 October 2015].

35. Shamah, D. (2015) "Gaza 'porn star video' spread malware in Israel, says report" (on net), 16 February, http://www.timesofisrael.com/gaza-porn-star-video-spread-malware-in-israel-says-report/ [accessed: 23 October 2015]

36. Dahms, T. (2014) "Molerats, here for Spring!" (on net), 2 June, https://www.fireeye.com/blog/threat-research/2014/06/molerats-here-for-spring.html [accessed: 23 October 2015].

37. Bennett, J. T. & Villeneuve, N. (2014) "XtremeRAT: nuisance or threat?" (on net), 19 February, https://www.fireeye.com/blog/threat-research/2014/02/xtremerat-nuisance-or-threat.html [accessed: 23 October 2015].

38. See for example: Kaspersky Lab (2015) *The Desert Falcons Targeted Attacks*. Kaspersky Lab (on net), https://securelist.com/files/2015/02/The-Desert-Falcons-targeted-attacks.pdf, p. 4 [accessed: 7 April 2016].

39. Hough, E. D., Mead, N. R. & Stehney II, T. R. (2005) *Security Quality Requirements Engineering (SQUARE) Methodology*. November (CMU/SEI-2005-TR-009). Software Engineering Institute, Carnegie Mellon University.

40. Trend Micro Threat Research Team (2015) *Operation Arid Viper: Bypassing the*

Iron Dome (on net). Trend Micro, p. I (Introduction), http://www.trendmicro. co.uk/media/wp/operation-arid-viper-whitepaper-en.pdf [accessed: 11 April 2016].

41. Middle East Cyber Army Jaysh al-Sharq al-Awsaṭ al-Iliktrūnī (2015) Middle East Cyber Army Jaysh al-Sharq al-Awsaṭ al-Iliktrūnī [Facebook], 7 April, https://www.facebook.com/Middle.East.Cyber.Army.7/photos/pb.41308 4208853473.-2207520000.1454938911./421484504680110/?type=3&theater [accessed: 8 February 2016].

42. BlackRose (2012) *Marjaʿ Qarāṣinat Ghazza li-ḥaqn qawāʿid al-bayānāt* (*Manual of Gaza Hacker Team for Data-injection*), November.

43. Ibid: "Qirāʾatak li-al-kitāb tantaqil mubāshirahu ilā ṣaff al-muḥtarafīn", p. 4.

6. FROM THE NATION TO THE UMMA

1. Gaza Hacker Team (n.d.) "ihdāʾ li-al-shaʿb al-falasṭīnī: Injāzāt Farīq Qarāṣinat Ghazza" ["A dedication to the Palestinian people: the achievements of Gaza Hacker Team"], p. 7.

2. Ibid., p. 8.

3. Ibid., p. 6.

4. Ibid.

5. al-Jazeera (n.d.) "Mīthāq ḥarakat al-muqāwama al-islāmiyya (Ḥamās)" ["Charter of the Islamic Resistance Movement (Hamas)"] (on net), http:// www.aljazeera.net/specialfiles/pages/0b4f24e4-7c14-4f50-a831-ea2b6e73217d [accessed: 27 October 2015].

6. Ibid., p. 8.

7. Ibid.

8. For a brief overview of several hacked websites conducted by Gaza Hacker Team, see Zone-H: https://zone-h.org/archive/notifier=Gaza%20Hacker%20 Team/page=1?zh=1

9. Zone-H (2012) "Defacement of hasamba.co.il" (on net), 25 August, https:// zone-h.org/mirror/id/18255985 [accessed: 29 September 2014].

10. Oxford Dictionary of Islam (2015) "Rawafid". In: Esposito, J. L. (ed.) *Oxford Islamic Studies Online* (on net), 27 October, http://www.oxfordislamicstudies. com/article/opr/t125/e1985 [accessed: 27 October 2015].

11. mr.leon, personal communication, 10 March 2015: "al-islām lam yantashir bi-al-sayf".

12. Ibid.: "Dāʿish ṣanāʿa amrīkiyya wa gharbiyya li-tashwīh ṣūrat al-islām".

13. mr.leon, personal communication, 8 March 2015.

14. Parker, S. (2014) *Bertolt Brecht: A Literary Life*. London, New Delhi, New York, Sydney: Bloomsbury, p. 2.

15. AnonRRD (2015) "Please remove the phrase 'electronic holocaust', #OpIsrael does not mean that, our fight is for the Palestinian people" [Twitter], 7 April, https://twitter.com/AnonRRD/status/585394387661803520 [accessed: 8 April 2015].

16. #OpIsrael (2015) "To clarify, we at this account do not endorse to usage of the word Holocaust. We did not come up with 'Electronic Holocaust'". #OpIsrael" [Twitter], 7 April, https://twitter.com/Op_Israel/status/585461368851169280 [accessed: 8 April 2015].

17. BlackOps, personal communication, 4 April 2015.

18. Eznai (2016) "Ashba 7 KH" [Internet archive], 10 January, https://archive.org/details/Ashba7KH [accessed: 12 January 2016].

19. Lia, B. (2015) "The Islamic State (IS) and its mediatized barbarism" (on net), 14 March, https://newmeast.wordpress.com/2015/03/14/the-islamic-state-is-and-its-mediatized-barbarism/ [accessed: 27 October 2015].

20. Ibid.

21. I should note that the theory of Ibn Khattab's appeal is not mine, but was suggested to me in discussions with Anne Stenersen.

22. mr.leon, personal communication, 8 March 2015.

23. Casper (2010) "Jamiʿ kalimāt wazīr al-ḥarb fī dawlat al-islām al-shaykh Abū Hamza al-Muhājir" (on net), 15 February, http://gaza-hacker.cc/show-thread-t_5549.html [accessed: 16 October 2015]. The website is no longer accessible.

24. Casper (2009) "al-Furqān: [al-Iqtiḥāmāt afjaʿ] kalima li-al-shaykh Abī Muḥ ammad al-ʿAdnānī – Ḥaff" (on net), 1 November, http://gaza-hacker.net/cc/showthread-t_42555.html [accessed: 16 March 2015]. The website is no longer accessible.

25. Casper (2010) "Jamiʿ kalimāt wazīr al-ḥarb fī dawlat al-islām al-shaykh Abū Hamza al-Muhājir" (on net), 15 February, http://gaza-hacker.cc/showthread-t_5549.html [accessed: 16 October 2015]. The website is no longer accessible.

26. mr.leon, personal communication, 15 March 2015.

27. Coleman, G. (2014) *Hacker, Hoaxer, Whistleblower, Spy: The Many Faces of Anonymous*. London, New York: Verso Books, p. 174.

28. Gaza Hacker Team forum front page (n.d.), http://gaza-hacker.net/cc [accessed: 26 September 2014 The website is no longer accessible.

29. Zone-H (2012) "Defacement of hasamba.co.il" (on net), 25 August, https://zone-h.org/mirror/id/18255985 [accessed: 29 September 2014].

30. "lā ʾilāha ʾilla Allāh, wa Muḥammad rasūl Allāh" ["There is no God but God, and Muhammad is his prophet"].

31. Zone-H (2012) "Defacement of ybcreative.co.il" (on net), 28 July, http://zone-h.org/mirror/id/18151204 [accessed: 29 September 2014].

32. Zone-H (2013) "Defacement of mamtakim4u.co.il" (on net), 25 February, http://zone-h.org/mirror/id/19395494 [accessed: 29 September 2014].

33. Zone-H (2012) "Defacement of asia-construction.co.il" (on net), 14 June, http://zone-h.org/mirror/id/17900790 [accessed: 29 September 2014].

34. Zone-H (2012) "Defacement of your-smile.co.il" (on net), 17 November, http://zone-h.org/mirror/id/18608836 [accessed: 29 September 2014].

35. Pape, R. (2005) *Dying to Win: The Strategic Logic of Suicide Bombing*. New York: Random House Publishing Group, p. 67.

36. Ibid., p. 4.

37. "al-ḥarb mustamirra li-ākhir sahyūnī ʿalā arḍ Falasṭīn al-ḥabība": Zone-H (2012) "Defacement of hasamba.co.il" (on net), 25 August, https://zone-h.org/mirror/id/18255985 [accessed: 29 September 2014].

38. ʿUmar al-ʿUmūr (2013) "'ājil ::: risāla min Qarāṣinat Ghazza li-al-ʿaddū al-sahyūnī … al-rijāʾ al-nashar" ("Urgent ::: message from Gaza Hacker Team to the Zionist enemy … Please share" [YouTube], 8 April, https://www.youtube.com/watch?v=hi9Yd3RxLyQ [accessed: 18 March 2015]. As Gaza Hacker Team in the interviews was asked if they had any political manifesto or ideology, they referred to this YouTube-video: mr.leon, personal communication, 10 September 2014.

39. Ibid.: "wa-innanā bi-qarāṣinat Ghazza natawāʿiḍ al-ʿadū al-isrāʾīlī ihāya ḥaṣala ʿalayhi mabtruhin lil-asīrī Sāmir al-ʿIsāwī".

40. McCants, W. (2015) *The ISIS Apocalypse: the History, Strategy, and Doomsday Vision of the Islamic State*, New York: St. Martin's Press, p. 56.

41. mr.leon 2014, pers. comm., 10 September.

42. Zone-H (2012) "Defacement of education.go.ug" (on net), 17 July, http://zone-h.org/mirror/id/18095314 [accessed: 29 September 2014].

43. Key to Islam (n.d.) "Introduction: the key to understanding Islam" (on net), http://www.thekeytoislam.com/en/ [accessed: 13 March 2015].

44. Wade, F. (2012) "Burma 'creating humanitarian crisis' with displacement camps in Arakan" (on net), 13 July, http://www.theguardian.com/world/2012/jul/13/burma-humanitarian-crisis-rohingya-arakan [accessed: 27 October 2015].

45. Zone-H (2012) "Defacement of ministryofinformation.gov.mm/administrator" (on net), 17 July, https://www.zone-h.org/mirror/id/18096067 [accessed: 29 September 2014].

46. Hegghammer, T. (2009) "Jihadi-Salafis or revolutionaries? On religion and politics in the study of militant Islamism". In: Meijer, R. (ed.) *Global Salafism: Islam's New Religious Movement*. London: C. Hurst & Co., p. 254.

47. Ibid., p. 263.

48. I should note that the comparison is not mine and was made by Thomas Hegghammer. Ibid., p. 259.

7.   ISLAMIC JIHAD AND HAMAS: THE PALESTINIAN CYBER-BRIGADES

1.   Hamas member 2, personal communication, 29 October 2014.
2.   Hamas member 1, personal communication, 29 October 2014.
3.   Ibid.
4.   Bunt, G. (2005) "Defining Islamic interconnectivity". In: Cooke, M. & Lawrence, B. B. (eds.) *Muslim Networks From Hajj to Hip Hop*. Chapel Hill, London: The University of North Carolina Press, p. 245.
5.   Abu Amer, A. (2015) "Hamas' cyber battalions take on Israel" (on net), 29 July, http://www.al-monitor.com/pulse/originals/2015/07/palestine-israel-internet-cyber-war-hacking.html [accessed: 4 November 2015].
6.   Ibid.
7.   Ruef, A., Shakarian, J. & Shakarian, P. (2013) *Introduction to Cyber-Warfare: A Multidisciplinary Approach*. Waltham: Syngress, Elsevier, pp. 39–40.
8.   Ibid.
9.   Žižek, S. (2009) *Violence: Six Sideways Reflections*. London: Profile Books, p. 65.
10.   al-Madhoun, O. (2008) "Islamic Jihad's cyber-war brigade" (on net), 17 June, http://www.menassat.com/?q=en/news-articles/3966-islamic-jihad-s-cyber-war-brigades [accessed: 4 November 2015].
11.   Main representative of Islamic Jihad West Bank, personal communication, 16 November 2014.
12.   Ayyoub, A. (2013) "Iran top backer of Palestinian Islamic Jihad" (on net), 9 January, http://www.al-monitor.com/pulse/originals/2013/01/palestinian-islamic-jihad.html# [accessed: 4 November 2015].
13.   Ingersoll, G. (2012) "REPORT: Jihadi hackers email Israel's military 'Tel Aviv will be a ball of fire'" (on net), 19 November, http://www.businessinsider.com/islamic-hackers-email-israel-military-2012-11 [accessed: 4 November 2015].
14.   Ackerman, G. & Abu Ramadan, S. (2012) "Israel wages cyber war with Hamas" (on net), 21 November, http://www.independent.co.uk/news/world/middle-east/israel-wages-cyber-war-with-hamas-8339519.html [accessed: 2 January 2016].
15.   Pollowitz, G. (2014) "Hamas wages cyber war on Domino's Pizza in Israel" (on net), 14 July, http://www.nationalreview.com/feed/382660/hamas-wages-cyber-war-dominos-pizza-israel-greg-pollowitz [accessed: 4 November 2015].
16.   Ibid.
17.   Gat, A. (2014) "Israeli hackers launch a 'proportionate response' to Hamas' cyber intifada" (on net), 20 July, http://www.geektime.com/2014/07/20/israeli-hackers-launch-a-proportionate-response-to-hamas-cyber-intifada/ [accessed: 4 November 2015].

18. Main representative of Islamic Jihad West Bank, personal communication, 16 November 2014.

19. Scott-Heron, G. (n.d.) "The revolution will not be televised" (on net), http://www.afropoets.net/gilscottheron2.html [accessed: 5 April 2016].

20. Hamas member 1, personal communication, 29 October 2014.

21. Main representative of Islamic Jihad West Bank, personal communication, 16 November 2014.

22. Ayyoub, A. (2013) "Iran top backer of Palestinian Islamic Jihad" (on net), 9 January, http://www.al-monitor.com/pulse/originals/2013/01/palestinian-islamic-jihad.html# [accessed: 4 November 2015].

23. Kronenfeld, S. & Siboni, G. (2014) "Developments in Iranian cyber warfare, 2013–2014" (on net), 3 April, http://www.inss.org.il/index.aspx?id=4538&articleid=6809 [accessed: 4 November 2015].

24. Halper, J. (2015) *The War Against the People: Israel, the Palestinians and Global Pacification*. London: Pluto Press, p. 47.

25. Ibid., p. 69.

26. Ibid., p. 137.

27. Cook, J. (2013) "Israel's booming secretive arms trade" (on net), 16 August, http://www.aljazeera.com/indepth/features/2013/08/201381410565517125.html [accessed: 4 November 2015].

28. Shamah, D. (2014) "Qatari tech helps Hamas in tunnels, rockets: expert" (on net), 31 July, http://www.timesofisrael.com/qatari-tech-helps-hamas-in-tunnels-rockets-expert/ [accessed: 4 November 2015].

29. D'Souza, D. (2006) "What's great about America" (on net), 23 February, http://www.heritage.org/Research/Reports/2006/02/Whats-Great-About-America [accessed: 5 April 2016].

30. Shamah, D. (2014) "Qatari tech helps Hamas in tunnels, rockets: expert" (on net), 31 July, http://www.timesofisrael.com/qatari-tech-helps-hamas-in-tunnels-rockets-expert/ [accessed: 4 November 2015]..

31. Guest (2013) "KDMS – crawl out from under the rocks" (on net), 11 October, http://pastebin.com/01iaU9z4 [accessed: 4 November 2015].

32. mr.leon, personal communication, 28 September 2014: "Lā yūjad faraq min al-Ḍiffa… Mithl Farīq Ghaḍab Falasṭīn lākin alān mushāghil al-ḥayyā faraqthum" ("There is no team from the West Bank… Like team Anger of Palestine, but they are not pursuing their social lives").

33. mr.leon, personal communication, 11 September 2014: "Fī hādhā al-ṣayf kān ikhtirāqatnā ḍaʿīfa jiddan" ("Our attacks were really weak this summer").

34. Bamford, J. (2014) "Israel's N.S.A. scandal" (on net), 16 September, http://www.nytimes.com/2014/09/17/opinion/israels-nsa-scandal.html?ref=opinion&_r=0 [accessed: 4 November 2015].

35. Main representative of Islamic Jihad West Bank, personal communication, 16 November 2014.

36. Shafei, F. (2015) "Gaza's cybercriminals get rich hacking Internet-based phone lines" (on net), 28 August, http://www.al-monitor.com/pulse/originals/2015/08/gaza-rafah-hacking-phone-calls.html# [accessed: 4 November 2015].

37. Ibid.

38. Haury, A. C. (2012) "10 of the most costly computer viruses of all time" (on net), 24 May, http://www.investopedia.com/financial-edge/0512/10-of-the-most-costly-computer-viruses-of-all-time.aspx [accessed: 14 November 2015].

39. al-Ghoul, A. (2013) "Credit card fraud goes unpunished in Gaza" (on net), 20 June, http://www.al-monitor.com/pulse/originals/2013/06/gaza-credit-card-fraud-electronic-warfare.html# [accessed: 4 November 2015].

40. See for example: Hobsbawm, E. (2001) *Bandits*. London: Weidenfeld & Nicolson.

41. Salah, H. (2014) "Gaza hackers prepare for next assault on Israel" (on net), 20 February, http://www.al-monitor.com/pulse/originals/2014/02/gaza-hackers-cyberwarfare-israel.html# [accessed: 4 November 2015].

42. mr. leon, personal communication, 28 September 2014: "Naḥnu bi-shakl ʿāmm sāʿadnā jamīʿ al-hākkir al-ʿarabī min khilāl al-durūs wa al-durrawāt ʿalā taṭwīr mahārāthum fī ikhtirāq wa waḍʿ turuq jadīda".

43. Quoted in: Shafei, F. (2015) "Gaza's cybercriminals get rich hacking Internet-based phone lines" (on net), 28 August, http://www.al-monitor.com/pulse/originals/2015/08/gaza-rafah-hacking-phone-calls.html [accessed: 04 November 2015].

44. This must not be confused with the term "honeypot" used in computing which is used to detect unauthorized use of information systems.

45. Krebs, B. "Malware spy network targeted Israelis, Palestinians" (on net), 12 November, http://krebsonsecurity.com/2012/11/malware-spy-network-targeted-israelis-palestinians/ [accessed: 4 November 2015].

8. DOES MATTER REALLY MATTER? PALESTINIAN AMBIVALENCE ABOUT ELECTRONIC JIHAD

1. al-Aqsa Martyrs' Brigade militant, personal communication, 15 October 2014.

2. Ibid.

3. Ibid.

4. Ibid.

5. Ibid.

6. PFLP and PLC member, personal communication, 9 September 2014.

7. al-Aqsa Martyrs' Brigade militant, personal communication, 15 October 2014.

8.   PFLP and PLC member, personal communication, 9 September 2014.
9.   Cambridge Dictionaries Online (n.d.) "Object" (on net), https://dictionary.cambridge.org/dictionary/english/object?a=british [accessed: 4 November 2015].
10. Leonardi, P. (2010) "Digital materiality? How artifacts without matter, matter" (on net), *First Monday – Peer-Reviewed Journal on the Internet*, vol. 15 (6), http://firstmonday.org/ojs/index.php/fm/article/view/3036/2567 [accessed: 4 November 2015].
11. Ibid.
12. PFLP and PLC member 2014, personal communication, 9 September.
13. Ravid, B. (2012) "PA president: as long as i am in power, there will be no third intifada" (on net), 1 November, http://www.haaretz.com/israel-news/pa-president-as-long-as-i-am-in-power-there-will-be-no-third-intifada-1.473852 [accessed: 4 November 2015].
14. al-Aqsa Martyrs' Brigade militant, personal communication, 15 October 2014.
15. Ibid.
16. Press TV Documentaries (2014) "At the heart of the siege: Hacker Force" (on net), 31 October, http://www.presstvdoc.com/Default/Detail/12951 [accessed: 4 November 2015], 12:27–13:00.
17. Abufarha, N. (2009) *The Making of a Human Bomb. An Ethnography of Palestinian Resistance*. Durham, London: Duke University Press, p. 80.
18. Jamāl Jumaʿ, personal communication, 9 November 2014.
19. Ibid.
20. Ibid.
21. Ibid.

9.   A CONTINUATION OF THE ARMED STRUGGLE?

1.   Dahan, M. (2013) "Hacking for the homeland: patriotic hackers versus hacktivists". In: Hart, D. (ed.) Proceedings of the 8th International Conference on Information Warfare and Security ICIW-2013. International Conference on Information Warfare and Security. Denver, Colorado, 25–26 March 2013. Reading, UK: Academic Conferences and Publishing International Limited.
2.   Quoted in: Darweish, M. & Rigby, A. (2015) *Popular Protest in Palestine: The Uncertain Future of Unarmed Resistance*. London: Pluto Press, p. 76.
3.   See for example: Gilbert, D. (2013) "WhatsApp, AVG and Alexa hacked by pro-Palestinian KDMS Team hackers" (on net), 8 October, http://www.ibtimes.co.uk/KDMS Team-pro-palistinian-hackers-whatsapp-avg-512269 and Meusers, R. (2013) "Website-Umleitung: WhatsApp, AVG und Avira von Hackern angegriffen" (on net), 9 October, http://www.spiegel.de/netzwelt/

web/server-von-whatsapp-und-antiviren-herstellern-gehackt-a-926872.html [both accessed: 12 November 2015].

4. There are several ways to describe the activities of hackers, where some are described as white hat hackers (ethical hacker to ensure web security), black hat hackers (hacker violating security, often for the sake of mischief) and lastly the grey hat hacker (hacker whose activities fall between the white and black hat hacker often acting illegally but with good intentions).

5. Doxing (abbreviation of documents) is a term used to describe the act of researching and finding personal identifiable information about groups or individuals and publishing them. This includes public databases, social media and sometimes also hacking.

6. KDMS Team, personal communication, 17 November 2014.

7. KDMS Team, personal communication, 21 December 2014.

8. Ibid.

9. Ibid.

10. KDMS Team, personal communication, 17 November 2014.

11. Zone-H (2013) "Defacement of bitdefender.com" (on net), 12 October, http://www.zone-h.org/mirror/id/20965099 [accessed: 12 December 2014].

12. KDMS Team, personal communication, 21 December 2014.

13. Cluley, G. (2013) "AVG and Avira anti-virus websites attacked by pro-Palestinian hackers" (on net), 8 October, https://grahamcluley.com/2013/10/avg-website-palestinian-hackers/ [accessed: 12 November 2015.

14. Darweish, M. & Rigby, A. (2015) *Popular Protest in Palestine: The Uncertain Future of Unarmed Resistance*. London: Pluto Press, p. 159.

15. Ibid., p. 82.

16. Peteet, J. (1996) "The writings on the walls: the graffiti of the Intifada". *Cultural Anthropology*, vol. 11 (2), p. 140.

17. Darweish, M. & Rigby, A. (2015) *Popular Protest in Palestine: The Uncertain Future of Unarmed Resistance*. London: Pluto Press, p. 7.

18. Dahan, M. (2013) "Hacking for the homeland: patriotic hackers versus hacktivists". In: Hart, D. (ed.) *Proceedings of the 8th International Conference on Information Warfare and Security ICIW-2013*. International Conference on Information Warfare and Security. *Denver, Colorado, 25–26 March 2013*. Reading: Academic Conferences and Publishing International Limited, p. 54.

19. Ibid., p. 55.

20. Ibid., p. 54.

21. Žižek, S. (2011) *Did Somebody Say Totalitarianism? Five Interventions in the (Mis)Use of a Notion*. London, New York: Verso Books, p. 131.

22. Jordan, T. & Taylor, P. A. (2004) *Hacktivism and Cyberwars: Rebels with a Cause?* New York, London: Routledge Taylor & Francis, p. 68.

23. Ibid.
24. Ibid., p. 69.
25. Ibid., p. 26.
26. Ibid.
27. Hopkins, N. (2013) "MI5 chief's criticism of Snowden and the Guardian is hardly unexpected" (on net), 9 October, http://www.theguardian.com/uk-news/2013/oct/09/mi5-chief-snowden-guardian-andrew-parker [accessed: 12 November 2015].
28. Palfrey, J. (2010) "Four phases of Internet regulation". *Social Research*, vol. 77 (3), p. 992.
29. Bender, J. (2014) "Israel: cyber is a bigger revolution in warfare than gunpowder" (on net), 4 February, http://www.businessinsider.com/the-internet-is-the-next-battlefield-2014-2?IR=T [accessed: 12 November 2015].
30. Deibert, R. J. (2003) "Black code: censorship, surveillance, and the militarization of cyberspace". *Millenium – Journal of International Studies*, vol. 32 (3), p. 518.
31. Caspit, B. (2015) "IDF to unify cyber warfare units" (on net), 18 June, http://www.al-monitor.com/pulse/originals/2015/06/israel-idf-cyber-intelligence-new-unit-eisenkot-war-future.html [accessed: 12 November 2015].
32. Halper, J. (2015) *The War Against the People: Israel, the Palestinians and Global Pacification*. London: Pluto Press, p. 116.
33. Kerr, D. (2014) "How Israel and Hamas weaponized social media" (on net), 13 January, http://www.cnet.com/news/how-israel-and-hamas-weaponized-social-media/ [accessed: 12 November 2015].
34. Ibid.
35. Ravid, B. (2013) "Prime Minister's Office recruiting students to wage online Hasbara battles" (on net), 13 August, http://www.haaretz.com/israel-news/.premium-1.541142?date=1447338665976 [accessed: 12 November 2015].
36. Deibert, R. J. (2003) "Black code: censorship, surveillance, and the militarization of cyberspace". *Millenium – Journal of International Studies*, vol. 32 (3), p. 518.

10. FINAL THOUGHTS

1. Jordan, T. & Taylor, P. A. (2004) *Hacktivism and Cyberwars: Rebels with a Cause?* New York, London: Routledge Taylor & Francis Group, pp. 74–75.
2. Hiluxanon (2012) "Anonymous #OpIsrael" [YouTube], 17 November, https://www.youtube.com/watch?v=q760tsz1Z7M [accessed: 17 November 2015].
3. Kashyap, P. (2013) "Major list of Israeli websites and leaked data which have been defaced for #OpIsrael (updated)" (on net), 6 April, http://www.hackers

newsbulletin.com/2013/04/major-list-of-israel-websites-which.html [accessed: 17 November 2015].

4. LeakSource (2013) "#OpIsrael: hackers of the world uniting forces for massive cyber attack on Israel" (on net), 10 March, http://leaksource.info/2013/03/10/opisrael-hackers-of-the-world-uniting-forces-for-massive-cyber-attack-on-israel/ [accessed: 17 November 2015].

5. Gaza Hacker Team (n.d.) "TKL: maʿlūmāt ʿannī" ("TKL: information about me") (on net), http://gaza-hacker.net/cc/member-u_22361.html [accessed: 17 November 2015]. The website is no longer accessible.

6. Gaza Hacker Team (n.d.) "ehabneo: rasāʾil al-zuwwār" ("ehabneo: visitors' messages") (on net), http://gaza-hacker.net/cc/member-u_17723.html [accessed: 17 November 2015]. The website is no longer accessible.

7. Gaza Hacker Team (n.d.) "Mr_AnarShi-T: rasāʾil al-zuwwār" ("Mr_AnarShi-T: visitors' messages") (on net), http://gaza-hacker.net/cc/member-u_17661.html [accessed: 17 November 2015]. The website is no longer accessible.

8. Gaza Hacker Team (n.d.) "mr.stalin: rasāʾil al-zuwwār" ("mr.stalin: visitors' messages") (on net), http://gaza-hacker.net/cc/member-u_10847.html [accessed: 17 November 2015]. The website is no longer accessible.

9. Zone-H (2012) "defacement of eyaltako.com" (on net), 29 August, https://zone-h.org/mirror/id/18271710?zh=1 [accessed: 3 October 2014].

10. Gaza Hacker Team (n.d.) "BlackRose: rasāʾil al-zuwwār" ("BlackRose: visitors' messages") (on net), http://gaza-hacker.net/cc/member-u_17559.html [accessed: 17 November 2015]. The website is no longer accessible.

11. Gaza Hacker Team (n.d.) "Th-Mx: rasāʾil al-zuwwār" ("Th-Mx: visitors' messages") (on net), http://www.gaza-hacker.net/cc/member-u_10531.html [accessed: 17 November 2015]. The website is no longer accessible.

12. Gaza Hacker Team (n.d.) "HANINE: rasāʾil al-zuwwār" ("HANINE: visitors' messages") (on net), http://gaza-hacker.net/cc/member-u_18793.html [accessed: 17 November 2015]. The website is no longer accessible.

13. Gaza Hacker Team (n.d.) "Micha: maʿlūmāt ʿannī" ("Micha: information about me") (on net), http://gaza-hacker.net/cc/member-u_11764.html [accessed: 17 November 2015]. The website is no longer accessible.

14. Gaza Hacker Team (n.d.) "zaradusht: rasāʾil al-zuwwār" ("zaradusht: visitors' messages") (on net), http://www.gaza-hacker.net/cc/member-u_23023.html [accessed: 17 November 2015]. The website is no longer accessible.

15. Gaza Hacker Team (n.d.) "aywanvictori: rasāʾil al-zuwwār" ("aywanvictori: visitors' messages") (on net), http://gaza-hacker.net/cc/member-u_13543.html [accessed: 17 November 2015]. The website is no longer accessible.

16. Gaza Hacker Team (n.d.) "llord: rasāʾil al-zuwwār" ("llord: visitors' messages") (on net), http://www.gaza-hacker.net/cc/member-u_26569.html [accessed: 17 November 2015]. The website is no longer accessible.

17. mr.leon, personal communication, 10 September 2014: "shay' akīd anna shabakat al-intirnit jaʿalat al-ʿālam qarriya ṣaghīra".

18. Ibid: "wa al-jānib al-akthar ahamiyya huwwa tajmaʿ al-hākkir al-ʿarabī wa al-ʿālamī li-hadaf wa al-istifāda min khibrāthim li-ikhtirāqt yumkin al-istifāda minhā wa īṣāl risāla min khilālhā".

19. al-Akhbār (2010) "al-Jihād al-Iliktrūnī min al-Azhar ilā ʿal-Qāʿida' ("Electronic Jihad from al-Azhar to al-Qaeda") (on net), 23 December, https://www.al-akhbar.com/node/443 [accessed: 4 January 2016].

20. Ibid.

21. Boccolini, H. (2009) "Morocco: hackers target Israeli websites to protest over Gaza" (on net), 16 January, http://www1.adnkronos.com/AKI/English/Security/?id=3.0.2916686513 [accessed: 4 January 2016].

22. Arab Times (2009) "Fatwā Saʿūdiyya Ṭāzija … Ṭāliʿa min al-Farn al-Yawm … al-Jihād al-Iliktrūnī Ḍidd al-Mawāqiʿ al-Iliktrūniyya al-Isrāʾīliyya Ḥarām wa Mamnūʿ" ("New Saudi Arabian fatwa … from al-Furn al-Yawm … Electronic Jihad against Israeli websites are unlawful and forbidden") (on net), 19 April, http://www.arabtimes.com/portal/news_display.cfm?Action=& Preview=No&nid=3781&a=112/17 [accessed: 4 January 2016].

23. Ṭālib al-Masʿūdī (2009) al-Jihād al-Iliktrūnī Ḍidd al-Mawāqiʿ al-Ṣahyūniyya Ghayr Jāʾiz !! Fatwā Ṣāliḥ al-Fawzān [al-Ghadīr Forum], 20 April, http://www.room-alghadeer.net/vb/showthread.php?t=15924 [accessed: 4 January 2016].

24. Anwār 88: Ibid.

25. Islam (2009) Ayḍan al-Jihād al-Iliktrūnī Muḥarram …ʿUḍḍū Hīʾat Kubbār al-ʿUlamāʾ fī al-Saʿūdiyya: Ikhtirāq wa Tadmīr al-Mawāqiʿ al-Iliktrūniyya al-Yahūdiyya "Lā Yajūz"!! [al-Quds talk forum], 18 April, http://www.alqudstalk.com/forum/showthread.php?t=1505 [accessed: 4 January 2016].

26. FireEye (2014) Regional advanced threat report: Europe, Middle East and Africa 1H2014. Milpitas, California: FireEye, p. 18.

27. Harel, A. (2013) "Israel's enemies are able to launch major cyber attack, defense expert says" (on net), 9 June, http://www.haaretz.com/israel-news/.premium-1.528588?date=1451903680278 [accessed: 4 January 2016].

28. Harman, D. (2014) "Cyber-defenders warn: Israel vulnerable to attack" (on net), 28 December, http://www.haaretz.com/world-news/.premium-1.633845 [accessed: 4 January 2016].

29. Dalton, W. (2012) "Israel–Gaza ceasefire takes hold, but will cyber-war relent?" (on net), 23 November, http://www.itproportal.com/2012/11/23/israel-gaza-ceasefire-takes-hold-but-will-cyber-war-relent/#ixzz3w6QTSgY9 [accessed: 4 January 2016].

EPILOGUE

1. Rogaway, P. (2015) "The moral character of cryptographic work". Asiacrypt 2015. Auckland, New Zealand, 2 December, p. 1.[a

2. Kelly, K. (1996) "The Electronic Hive: Embrace It". In: Kling. R. (ed.) *Computerization and Controversy: Value Conflicts and Social Changes*. San Diego, San Francisco, New York, Boston, London, Sydney, Tokyo: Morgan Kaufmann, p. 78

INDEX

conflict correlation, 58; Islamic Law permissible, 174; 'keeping pace with' Israel, 116; non-state actors, 178; stages of, 6

hacktivism, Palestinian, 1-3, 13; al-Aqsa Brigade non-prioritized, 135; fatwa against, 17; internationalization of, 177; Palestinian opponents/sceptics, 133-6 popular resistance element, 10, 161;

hacktivists: border transgressing, 172; characteristics of, 140; clear political purpose, 7; educated Palestinian, 170

Haifa tunnel, security cameras hacked, 77

Halper, Jeff, 41, 45, 121, 164

Hamas, 24, 70-2, 89, 103-4, 126, 128-30, 137, 142, 149, 161; cyber units, 81, 162, 165; cyber-department, 56; electronic defense units, 114, 166, 'electronic jihad' call, 2; electronic warfare units, 59, 112, 136; -Fatah rivalry, 53; -Fatah unification process, 141; first suicide bomb, 26; Gaza Hacker Team different, 90; help from abroad, 120; nationalist goals, 24; PR, 111;-Qatar cooperation, 122; TV station Israel hacked, 58; website pornography hacked, 113

Hamza Abu al-Hayja, assassination of, 114

HANINE', Lebanon hacker, 172

Hannibal, pro-Israeli hacker, 2

Harb, Ramez, Israel assassinated, 118

Hass, Amira, 27

Hegghammer, Thomas, 108

Hertog, Steffen, 59

Hewlett-Packard, 42-3

high-tech sector, Israel: cluster development, 43; defense spending link, 39

Hiluxxanon, YouTube video, 171

Hizb al-Sha'b, 143

Hizb al-Tahrir al-Islami, da'wa' practice, 143

Hizbollah: rise of, 24; website Israeli hacked, 56

Hobsbawm, E., 'social bandit' thesis, 127

Holocaust, the, 19

homeland security, Israel high-tech sector, 43

'house cleansing', 71

Ibn Khattab, 99; classical jihadism symbol, 100

IDF, websites targeted, 171

Institute for National Security Studies, 121

Intel, Israel subsidy to, 41

International Court of Justice, 14

internet: 'activism, 7; borders transgressing, 48; commercialization prevention activity, 6; gender relations impact, 34; militarization of, 162-3; narrative discourse changing, 49-50; -Optimists, 5; pornography, 32, 36; religious authority criticisms, 176; intrastate conflicts, 176

Iran, 90, 164, 181; cyber brigades help, 120-1; nuclear facility cyber attacked, 60Oil Ministry malware targeted, 61

Iraq, 32; late internet introduction, 31

Islam Net, 94

Islamic Gateway World Wide Media Network, 57

Islamic network, 103

Islamic Revolution, Iran, 24

Islamic State, 93, 103, 177; propaganda used, 95

Islamic University of Gaza, 128

Islamist groups: electronic resistance use, 140; secular-nationalist goals, 104

Israel, 32; army 'cyber-branch', 164; boundary wall construction, 49; control tools, 139; cyber attacks on, 1; cyber-defenses, 180; Defense Force (IDF), *see below*; defense spending, 39; domain websites hacked, 57; Facebook defacements, 95; first ISP 1992, 46; ICT cluster, 38, 42; Kadima party website hacked, 67; legitimacy

non-questioning, 20; military–digital complex, 36-8; military-high-tech company close relation, 44-5; Ministry of Foreign Affairs hacked, 56; 1948 establishment, 16; normality disruption, 79, 156; Palestinian land-grabbing, 154; police, see below; Second Intifada militarization welcomed, 54; servers reputations damaged, 76; surveillance and identification system, 43;
Israeli Civil Administration, collaborators with, 71
Israeli Defense Force (IDF), 36-8, 44-5; 'cyber-branch', 164; security network, 57social media student recruiting, 165; soldiers addresses hacked, 117; Twitter account hacked, 80; vulnerable Palestinians monitoring, 114; website hacked, 171
Israeli National Information Security Authority, 180
Israeli police: computers compromised 2012, 66; GHT hacked, 81; 'Xtreme Rat' use against, 83
Israeli Sapir College, 157
#'IsraelUnderFire', 49
Issawi, Samir, 106
al-Istishhadi, 15; emergence of, 53
Izz al-Din al-Qassam Brigade, 69, 115, 120, 136, 165

J.P. Morgan Chase, web site hacked, 58
Ja'bari, Ahmad, Israel assassination of, 164
Jabhat al-Nusra, 103
Jama'at al-Tawhid wa al-Jihad, 106
Jaradat, Arafat, death of, 104
Jawwal, Palestine telecoms company, 47
Jerusalem attacks, 2013, 112
Jihadi John, Anon Ghost image use, 95
jihadism, Salafi, 88, 108 jihadis' media attention competition, 99

Jobs, Steve, 126
Joffe, Rodney, 58
Jordan, 32; high literacy rate, 33; Irbid District, 19; King Hussein, 18, 71
Jordan, T., 6, 9, 160
Judaism-Zionism distinction, 87
Juma, Jamal, 144, 146

Kaplan, Robert D., 54
Karameh, Jordan 1968 victory, 18
KDMS Team (hackers), 3, 58, 69, 150, 155, 158, 160, 166, 178; capable, 154; international sites attacks, 151, 153; political party non-affiliation, 152
Kelly, Kevin, 5, 186
Kerr, Dara, 164
Khadr 'Adnan, 104
Khattab, Ibn, 168-9, 172
Khaybar, battle of, 91, 92
Khomeini, Ruhollah, 120
Kingsman: The Secret Service, 184
Kissinger, Henry, 122
Knesset: website hacked, 56; wiretapping of, claim, 133
knowledge transfer, Israeli military-ICT company, 44
Kovachi, Edward, 163
Kreiner, Erez, 180
Kuwait, 31-3, 178

Lebanon, 19, 32; high literacy rate, 33; PLO 1982 defeat, 19, 23 War 2006, 58
Leonardi, Paul, 137-8
Lia, Brynjar, 99
Libya, 32; high literacy rate, 33
Likud, hacked
'Nimu al-Iraq', 114
literacy levels-cyber development relation, 33
'Llord', Morocco, 172-3
Lockheed Martin Corporation, 121

MacAfee, 76
Maktoob, 33